The RIVER WELLAND, SHIPPING & MARINERS OF SPALDING

Keith Seaton

The History Press

To all those mariners of Spalding who sailed upon the seas both near and far who have long since departed this life:

THEY THAT GO DOWN TO THE SEA IN SHIPS that do business in great waters; These see the works of the LORD and his wonders in the deep. For He commandeth, and raiseth the stormy wind, which lifteth up the waves thereof. They mount up to the heaven, they go down again to the depths: their soul is melted because of trouble. They reel to and fro, and stagger like a drunken man, and are at their wits' end. Then they cry unto the LORD in their trouble, and He bringeth them out of their distresses. He maketh the storm a calm, so that the waves thereof are still. Then are they glad because they be quiet; so He bringeth them unto their desired haven.

(Psalms 107:23–30)

Cover illustrations: *Front:* The SS *Misterly*. *Back:* Pannell's boatyard. Both F. Parkinson, Spalding Gentlemen's Society Collection.

First published 2013

The History Press
The Mill, Brimscombe Port
Stroud, Gloucestershire, GL5 2QG
www.thehistorypress.co.uk

British Library Cataloguing in Publication Data.
A catalogue record for this book is available from the British Library.

ISBN 978 0 7524 9449 4

Typesetting and origination by The History Press
Printed in Great Britain

CONTENTS

Acknowledgements   4

Introduction   6

1   The River Welland   9

2   Welland History   22

3   Types of Vessel Using the Port of Spalding   46

4   Family History   53

5   Some Other Spalding Mariners   58

6   *Boston Ships Registers* 1824–92: Spalding and District

     Masters and Owners   85

7   Censuses and Directories   103

8   Shipping Memories of Some Spalding Residents   128

9   Shipping News from Local Newspapers   137

10   Spalding Shipwreck Society   161

11   Boatbuilders and Associated Industries   164

12   Into the Twentieth Century   174

     Bibliography   190

     Index   191

Acknowledgements

The author wishes to thank:

The president and council of the Spalding Gentlemen's Society (the Frank Parkinson photography glass-negative plate collection, postcard collection, reference books, etc.).

Lincolnshire Library Service Spalding (microfiche of *Lincolnshire Free Press* and *Lincoln, Rutland & Stamford Mercury*, censuses and reference books).

The Lincolnshire Archives (microfiche and books of *Boston Ships Registers*).

Mrs Kathleen Pell and Mr Roy Pell (photograph of William Henry Grassam and other information on the Grassam family).

Mr Tony Levesley and Mrs Heather Caswell (painting of the *Breeze*, photograph of Captain George Levesley and his Master's certificate).

Mr G. Arnold (copy of the postcard of the *Breeze*).

Mr Richard Walker (copy of the painting of John Turner 1771, information about his voyage with Commander George Vancouver on HMS *Discovery* and his later service in the Royal Navy and photograph of John Turner, 1839–1926).

Mr Geoff Dodd (the ledgers of Edward Fisher, blacksmith of the Chain Bridge Forge 1849–98 and also information from his reminiscences *Three Generations of Blacksmiths* and family photographs).

Mr Tom Smith of Whitton (photograph of the sloop *Walcot*).

Mrs Margaret Johnson (photographs of G.F. Birch senior and junior and Birch's vessels).

Mr Stewart E. Squires (copies of photographs of Wragg Marsh Wharf, as in his book *The Lincolnshire Potato Railways*).

Mr Stewart Ingle (copy of a painting of the sloop *Success*).

Mr Neil Pulling (photograph of *Jonsue*, 1982).

Mr Martin Brewster (photographs taken by Mr Roland Brewster of Coronation Channel sluice opening, 1953).

Mr David Hensman (the 1834 Welland Navigation by-laws).

Mr Robert Bester (modern photograph of the Chain Bridge Forge).

Mr Richard Buck for help with an author questionnaire and many other people for help, advice and encouragement to complete this book.

The History Press.

INTRODUCTION

When I started to research the Vine family history on the census pages, I also found lots of local surnames that were familiar to me that had been connected with shipping in the nineteenth century. When I was a boy and living in Albert Street I remember a Captain Hayes who lived at the top of the road nearest to the river. On the other side of the road was the home of the Levesley family; Captain George Levesley had been a witness at my great-great-grandfather's wedding. A little further down the road was Fern Cottage, where Captain Atkin had lived. The *Fern* was the name of one of the last sailing vessels to come up the river. In fact, so many local families had been connected to shipping that I decided to look further than my own family, as there did not seem to be any books focusing entirely on the

Paddling my first kayak on the River Welland, 1956.

history of the Welland, Spalding and shipping. This book is the result of several years of research. Many hours of my time have been spent searching the census records for vessels and mariners and their families, looking at the earlier microfilm copies of the *Spalding Free Press* and various directories at Spalding library, and reading many Lincolnshire history books. I have explored the River Welland from beyond Stamford to the sea, on the water where possible by boat or kayak, or on foot.

Some of the channels between Tallington and Market Deeping are now no more than shallow ditches, and apart from the two disused locks in the Deepings only a few traces of the other part of the Stamford Canal are to be found today.

I was born on 11 June 1939 at No. 24 Albert Street, Spalding, a second son to Ralph and Florence M. Seaton. The River Welland was at the top of the street beside Commercial Road, and from an early age I was attracted to the river. When I started school I crossed it every day via the Albert (Chain) Bridge.

The blacksmith Mr Banks 'Jim' Dodd would wind the bridge open to let G.F. Birch's barges through at high tides. Sometimes one or two children were allowed to stand on the bridge as it was swung round. When my grandfather Herbert Seaton retired at the end of the Second World War, we moved to No. 4 Commercial Road (the three-storey building on the right in the Chain Bridge picture below) to live at the bakery. Then I was

The Albert Bridge or Chain Bridge, which I crossed daily on my way to and from the Westlode Street School.

even closer to the river and we played on the banks and fished for eels with tots of worms. All the young boys living near the river had done this type of fishing for years and it was known as 'totting'. All that was needed was a long cane or brush pole and a length of string without a hook, a cork float, and a sinker of any small piece of metal. We would dig for large earthworms and thread them onto the string by pushing a darning needle into the front end of the worms and out the back to make a long line of worms. This was then doubled up and doubled up again to make a tot. Once it was cast into the water we waited until the cork was pulled under and then quickly pulled the tot out with the eel hanging onto it. They were slippery, slimy fish and difficult to handle, so they very often landed in the grass and were lost. Most of them were put back in the river anyway, unless they were large and could be sold for a few pennies to a local man named Mr Baker, who liked to eat them. A favourite place to fish was by the swinger, near to the top of Albert Street. This was a cut into the bank that allowed the ships and barges to be swung round so that they headed back downstream bow-first after they had unloaded cargo.

In 1947, after the thaw, the meltwaters coming downstream caused the river to overflow in parts of the town, and water came up to the top step of our cellar. The road at our back gate in Willow Walk was also flooded in parts where the water had come back up the road drains from the river.

It was not until later, when I had started to attend the Sir John Gleed Boys' School, that I found out my family connections with the river. Uncle Tom (my father's younger brother) showed me a photograph of great-grandfather John Henry Vine, taken on the deck of his vessel the *Breeze*. Unfortunately I have no idea what happened to this photograph, but I do have a copy of the postcard of the *Breeze* on the river at a mooring by Commercial Road which was taken in the late 1800s. John Henry Vine was grandmother Edith Ada Seaton's father.

1

THE RIVER WELLAND

Weland [*sic*], having its rise near Sibertoft in Northamptonshire, and taking in some petty streamlets, cometh at length to Market Deping, and St James Deping, where it enterth the fens, and burdeneth them with all the water and downfalls of part of Northampton, Leicester, Rutland, and Lincoln shires; whence passing to Crowland bridge, it divided itself into two branches; the one leading by South Eau towards Wisbeche, the other in a most slow course, to Spalding and Surfleet, where receiving the waters of Glen, it goes on to Fosse dyke stow, and so into Boston deep. (Sir William Dugdale, *The History of Imbanking and Drayning the Fens and Marshes, and of the Improvements Intended Thereby,* 1662)

Sibbertoft is close to the battlefield of Naseby, the site of the battle between the forces of King Charles I and the Roundhead army commanded by Thomas Fairfax, which ended with the defeat of the Royalists. This is where the River Welland rises up out of the ground from a spring and then flows onward to pass close to Husbands Bosworth.

It then passes through Market Harborough, gradually getting larger as it is fed from other small chalk streams, and occasionally dividing into two and then joining back together again further downstream. Its course from near Rockingham forms the border of the counties of Rutland and Northamptonshire until just before it reaches Stamford in Lincolnshire. Near Tinwell the River Chater joins the Welland, adding more water to it. I found another small spring rising out of the ground in a small wood at Kilthorpe Grange near Tixover while walking in the area some years ago.

The river is crossed by bridge at Duddington. A few miles north of here the large Rutland Water reservoir can now be found. Officially opened in 1976, it is one of the largest artificial lakes in the country. Some of the water in this reservoir is drawn from a pumping station on the north bank

River Welland, Market Harbrough, in a postcard postmarked 2 May 1908.

The river approaching Stamford, in a postcard from 1962.

at Stamford Meadows, just before the town of Stamford on the route to Spalding.

As it reaches Stamford the Welland now forms the border between Cambridgeshire and Lincolnshire. Here it passes under the A1, which in earlier times passed through the centre of the town. This caused much congestion as motor traffic increased. It is believed that the Roman Ermine

Street crossed the river at Stamford, giving the town its name – the elements 'stane' and 'ford' suggest a paved ford across a river.

After the three-arched St Martin's town bridge, the river passes the old wharf on the left, under the Albert Footbridge to Water Road, and then the park of Burghley House on the right. Continuing past a weir, it reaches the first lock of the Stamford Canal going downstream, Lock No. 12. The

Town Bridge, Stamford, in a Valentine's postcard from the 1900s.

Downriver from Stamford Bridge. (F. Parkinson, Spalding Gentlemen's Society collection)

old course of the river continues to the left – Hudd's Mill is on this part – before it crosses the River Gwash. Uffington Park, where some dry remains of the Stamford Canal can still be seen, is on the right.

Winding its way towards the Deepings it reaches Tallington, which marks the start of the Maxey Cut that diverts floodwaters around the Deepings to rejoin the Welland at a junction near Peakirk, where the Folly River and South Drain also join it. Here there are sluices feeding the streams that once supplied power to the watermills upstream from Market Deeping. The first of these takes water to West Deeping and Molecey's Mill, the second to Lolham and Maxey Mill. Between Molecey's Mill and the main road, formerly the A16 and now the A1175 the remains of the Stamford Canal can be seen. The Greatford Cut, which carries water from the West Glen, passes under the A1175 and joins the river before the two streams join again near to the new bridges on the A15 Market Deeping bypass to Peterborough. Before the old Market Deeping Bridge are the weir and the Market Deeping Mill next to the remains of Lock No. 3 of the Stamford Canal.

Passing through Market Deeping and Deeping Gate, the river comes to Deeping St James and the second lock, Briggin's or High Lock, and the weir before passing under the three-arched stone bridge.

Continuing on to Low Lock, which was No. 1 on the Stamford Canal system, the river winds along behind many new houses with riverside

River and Market Deeping Bridge.

Briggin's Lock and weir.

The Low Lock, Deeping St James, in a postcard from around 1900.

gardens and then into the countryside, passing under a railway bridge to the junction with the Maxey Cut near Peacock. At this point the river becomes navigable, but at some times of the year there is a large shoal of hard rock and gravel in the middle, close to the Deeping Nature Reserve, created by the removing of large quantities of sand and gravel. The extraction of sand

Crowland, Trinity Bridge, around 1900.

and gravel has been going on for many years from Deeping Langtoft Baston and Tallington. Since extraction has finished these sites have been given over to be used as nature reserves and water sports venues.

From here the river has been improved all the way to Spalding, with high banks to prevent flooding and Crowland now by-passed completely. Many years before, the river flowed to a junction with a branch of the River Nene. The monks of Crowland Abbey built the three-way triangular Trinity Bridge of Barnack stone over the junction of these two rivers between 1360 and 1390. No water flows underneath them now, but the bridge is maintained as a Scheduled Monument and Grade 1 listed structure.

From the road bridge over the river to the outskirts of Spalding is a distance of around 9 miles, with little of interest other than the waterfowl that inhabit the river. The breeding population, species and numbers are increased in the winter by the many migrant species from the northern continent that come to escape the Arctic climate.

Over the bank on the right are the Crowland Wash and Cowbit Wash. They were purposely flooded most winters for many years in order to relieve the river of water that otherwise would have flooded Spalding. In March 1947 the bank on the east side of Crowland Wash gave way and the farmland was flooded, with water flowing through and scouring out a large hole. To enable the bank to be repaired, a number of redundant army tanks with their gun turrets removed were put in and around the breach.

Winter wildfowl.

Tanks in the
breach at
Crowland
Wash, 1947.
(John Honnor
collection)

Cowbit Wash
flooded, around
1900. (Fenland
Pictures, Spalding
Free Press
Company Ltd)

Speed skater, Baston Fen, 1963.

Cowbit Wash flooded, around 1900. (Postcard, Spalding Free Press Company Ltd)

Most winters the river was frozen over and ice skating was a popular sport, with races being watched by crowds of people from near and far. The *London Illustrated News* reported that on Friday 26 December 1891 the Lincolnshire Skating Association, whose headquarters were at Spalding, held a grand race for its championship with a course of 10 miles along the River Welland – 5 miles to the Counter Drain station of the Bourne to Lynn Railway and back to Spalding. The winner was Tom Pickering of Cowbit Spalding who completed the course in thrity-nine minutes, seven seconds. In 1900 Walter Pridgeon won the championship, which was a distance of 1 mile raced around barrels on the Cowbit Wash. He was champion until 1933 when Bert Slater of Crowland won the title. Speed skaters that I remember are Doug Beba, Victor Smith and Alan Fisher from Moulton Chapel. Victor won for the first time in 1963 aged 20, beating the title-holder Jack Cary of Crowland and Alan Fisher, aged 17, who went on to win the race a total of ten times. I learned to skate on fen runners – metal blades fitted onto wooden shoe-sole-shaped blocks that were screwed and strapped onto my football boots after taking out the studs. Later I inherited my father's Norwegian racing skates, but I was never proficient enough to enter any races.

In later years the Wash at Tongue End (the Baston Fen Nature Reserve) was flooded from the River Glen to allow the Lincolnshire championship races to take place, but this practice ended in 1993 due to crippling insurance charges over public liability. It was pasture land for the most part, since crops would have been ruined when it was flooded, but since the Coronation Flood Relief Channel was built it is now mostly cultivated and producing valuable crops.

As we reach Spalding the view has changed since the next two photographs were taken. The cottages on the right are still there, with other houses also having been built. The mill was demolished in 1899 and the cottages on the right have also gone, replaced by a modern house and moorings with charging points for the local electric water-taxi boats.

The river after this point enters into metal pilings – put in during work after the floods of 1947 – up to the entrance of the Coronation Flood Relief Channel. This was completed in 1952 and officially opened in 1953, the year of the coronation of Queen Elizabeth II, by Sir Thomas Dugdale, Minister of Agriculture and Fisheries, on 24 September. After the opening of the Cowbit Road sluice gates the official party, including Alex West, chairman of the Welland Drainage Board, and Edwin Tavener, the chief engineer, travelled by barge to the Marsh Road sluice.

Although no longer tidal, the river through the town has not changed its course. However, the buildings on both sides along the road have changed.

The river at Locks Mill on the outskirts of Spalding. (F. Parkinson, Spalding Gentlemen's Society collection)

The river at Locks Mill at low tide, with children playing. (F. Parkinson, Spalding Gentlemen's Society collection)

The opening of the Cowbit Road sluice gates. (Photograph Mr R. Brewster, copyright Mr M. Brewster)

The official party on the barge. (Photograph Mr R. Brewster, copyright Mr M. Brewster)

The 1838 town bridge is still in place today. This photograph was taken when the river was tidal. (F. Parkinson, Spalding Gentlemen's Society collection)

The Coronation Channel sluice gates outfall to the tidal River Welland.

It is a conservation area now, so many of the older ones are protected, but some were unfortunately lost before this status was granted. The river passes through the town under the High Bridge and on towards the locks at Roman Bank where it becomes a tidal river again. Roman Bank is also where the Coronation Channel empties water into the Welland through the Marsh Road sluice gates, which open automatically when the channel reaches a certain level but only when the tide is going down.

Around 4½ miles downstream from this point are the outlets into the Welland through locks of the Vernatts Drain and the River Glen at Surfleet Seas End, where several yachts and motor vessels are moored up to landing stages by their owners to be used for pleasure trips into the Wash. From here to the Fosdyke Bridge is around another 3½ miles, passing by the Fosdyke Yacht Haven. Then the river is embanked for several more miles through reclaimed land until it finally reaches its outfall into the Wash.

2

WELLAND HISTORY

The Romans

We are led to believe that the Romans occupied land in the Welland valley in the second century AD, around the time that the Emperor Hadrian visited Britain. By drainage of the fens with navigable drains they were able to form many small settlements that produced crops that could then be transported by boat down these drains to the larger vessels on the Welland and onward to the military in the north and on the Continent. The largest of the waterways they were supposed to have built was the Car Dyke, which crossed over the River Nene near Peterborough and reached the River Witham within a few miles of Lincoln. If this was so it would also have had to cross over the Welland near the Deepings, but how this happened is unclear; I have not been able to find any accounts of the remains of aqueducts being found by archaeologists, for example. There are also differing opinions as to whether Car Dyke was for transport or for drainage. Another drain was the Westlode Drain, which was cut to help take some of the water from the Car Dyke to ease flooding of the fens.

Spalding at that time was an island or area high ground in the fen and some distance from the mouth of the River Welland, which had its outlet nearer to Deeping. To extend the river to Spalding the Romans built high banks around the Cowbit Wash. These are still in existence today, although they have been repaired many times. From Spalding past Cowbit to Brotherhouse Bar the road runs on top of them. The river itself now runs in a different place, due to later dredging and realignment. These banks were connected to the sea bank, which at that time stretched from around Wisbech to the Humber. Parts of a sea bank are still in existence today – the suggestively named Roman Bank from Moulton Seas End through to

Saracen's Head and other stretches of bank around the Wash – but they are thought to have been built in medieval times.

In recent years several sites around Spalding have been excavated by archaeologists before new dwellings have been given planning consent. In the course of this work, evidence has been found of a thriving Roman salt industry arranged close to the sea banks to make use of the brine. I spent two days taking part in field-walking exercises with archaeologists near Spalding at Willow Tree Fen, during which a saltern was found along with many small pieces of pottery dated to the Roman period, including Samian ware, locally made pottery and part of a handle from an amphora.

We are told that the Romans built a large stone bridge consisting of four arches over the Welland on the site of the present High Bridge. This Roman construction stood for 1,200 years and was known as the Great Bridge of Spalding although no archaeological evidence has been recorded that I can find. They found Spalding of great value as a port, enabling them to export cattle, sheep and other goods produced in the fens to their armies on the Continent. The Romans departed from Lincolnshire sometime around AD 420, but there is no written evidence to tell us when they left Spalding and no building remains have been found, as it is thought that most dwellings would have been made with light timber, clay, reeds and turves because of the lack of any local stone in the fens. As such, the only evidence of Roman occupation discovered here has been some pottery and coins.

Anglo-Saxons

After the Romans had gone, parts of Lincolnshire were occupied by Anglo-Saxon settlers from Europe. Many of them originally came to render military service helping to drive back the invading Picts and Scots in return for lands including some in the fens of South Lincolnshire. During this time of war the banks and drains were neglected and the fens were soon in as bad a state as they were previous to the Roman occupation.

Ninth to Eleventh Centuries

In these centuries the Danes invaded Lincolnshire with some of them possibly settling in the south of the county around Spalding. In 1051 Thorold of Buckenhale, Sheriff of Lincoln and brother of Godiva, Countess of Leicester, founded the priory and built the abbey at Spalding. Following the defeat of King Harold at Hastings in 1066, William the Conqueror's nephew and standard bearer, Ivo Tailbois, came to live in the area in 1071 and married Thorold's niece, the Countess Lucy. He was supposed to have had a castle in Spalding in the area that is now the Castle Sports Centre Playing Field but there are no remains of a castle to be seen today.

Twelfth Century

In the twelfth century Spalding was reliant on the navigability of the River Welland. It was a sub-port of Boston, which was a larger port even than London at this time. The outfall of the River Welland was near to Wykeham, and a vessel that was wrecked on the beach in 1140 was claimed by the prior for his own use as the owner of the manor and under Royal Charter.

Thirteenth Century

The priory suffered some losses from flooding in 1287. A great flood occurred on New Year's Day; several churches were destroyed and many men, women and children drowned.

Spalding, situated as it was at the mouth of the Welland, was a thriving seaport with many ships sailing over to Flanders with wool and woad to be used for dyeing the same. They then returned with cargoes of wines and luxuries for the monasteries of Spalding, Crowland, Deeping and Stamford. The ships were unloaded at Spalding onto barges, which proceeded up river as far as Stamford and returned with other cargo, including stone from Barnack that was used to build many of the churches that still stand in South Lincolnshire today.

The river was the only means of communication for Crowland, and most of its imports and exports had to come through Spalding, so the Abbot was anxious to keep Spalding under his jurisdiction. The roads were very poorly maintained and heavy loads such as stone could be transported more easily by water, with tidal streams meaning that the stone could be unloaded on the spot. Furthermore, many of the roads had tolls that made them expensive to use.

The Prior of Spalding from 1274 to 1294 was William of Littleport. He was succeeded by Clement Hatfield.

Fourteenth Century

Prior Clement Hatfield built his country residence, the manorial hall, in 1311. At the same time he had Wykeham chapel erected and dedicated to St Nicholas, the patron saint of sailors. At this time the chapel was close to the mouth of the River Welland. Hatfield built a wharf here for his own use, allowing vessels to unload cargoes of wine and other goods. The ships were small and both Surfleet and Fosdyke were named as ports, while Spalding had a considerable seagoing trade.

In 1326 Spalding was ordered to provide two ships with forty armed men, from the better ships of the town, to protect the coast and suppress piracy in the Wash. In 1332 the population of Spalding was about 3,000.

The drains and ditches had become defective through lack of repair, and the surrounding lands were often underwater. The town of Spalding was in danger of being submerged by the flow of the sea. The keepers of the ditches did not know who was responsible for their repair.

Wykeham Abbey and manorial hall.

Fifteenth Century

In 1433 the Abbot of Crowland, John Litlington, was to repair the banks around the Cowbit Wash. The Prior of Spalding, John Holland, agreed that Litlington could take from Spalding Fen to as near to Brotherhouse as was possible as much earth, sand and clay for making the bank as 100 boats could carry on the Welland, each boat containing six cartloads. The abbot broke his agreement and great damage was done by floods by 1439 because he had not repaired the banks.

On 24 November 1436 a severe frost commenced. It persisted until 10 February 1440, causing rivers all over England to be frozen over right up to the sea and the ships had to unload their cargoes onto wagons to be transported inland.

In the year of 1467 there was a great flood and all the area was underwater.

Sixteenth Century

After the dissolution of the monastery there was no one responsible for ordering and paying for the rivers and drains to be cleaned out and banks to be repaired, and soon their state was almost as bad as it had been in Saxon times. The rivers became choked up with silt and were unable to drain the waters from the high country, so the fens were flooded all year. In 1578 Queen Elizabeth I appointed commissioners to enquire into the cost and best way of draining the fens, but nothing was done during her reign:

> The Captain [Thomas Lovell] devoted his skill under a decree of the Commissioners of Sewers made at Spalding to affect the drainage of Deeping Fen, an area which had never been brought into the drainage system of the Great Level. His plans failed through the defects of the outfall of the Welland and afterwards Thomas, Earl of Exeter, endeavoured to make them effectual by conveying the Westlode and Deeping Fen waters by sluices and tunnels at Cowbit, under the Welland, into South Holland, works which so diverted the volume of water that below Spalding there was no river at all. The result of the Earl's works was that a river, which in former ages flowed with a part of the Nene through Crowland to Spalding, at the end of the 16th century brought water to the Isle of Ely. (*Fenland Notes and Queries* Vol. 5, 1901–03)

Seventeenth Century

On 21 June 1605 a particular inspection of the whole level was begun, and was certified as follows. First we repaired to the outfall to the sea at the meeting of the two rivers of Welland and Glen, where we found the outfall reasonably good. Thence to Cowhirne and Pikebridge and so to Spalding Bridge, in all which passage we found the river very defective in breadth and depth and from Cowhirne to Spalding Bridge a great bank lying on either side of the river. From Spalding Bridge to Willow Row end by Cowbit and Peakhill to Whitehouse, the river all along being defective, having a great elbow at Cowbit and Peakhill which much hindered its course to the outfall. (E.H. Gooch, *The History of Spalding*, 1940)

Between 1604 and 1616, James I ordered Admiral Sir William Monson to exterminate the pirates around the Wash, which he effectually did, greatly to the relief of the local mariners – though tradition says that some of our men were not averse to participating in this lucrative and fashionable mode of livelihood when the opportunity presented itself.

In 1618 the commissioners again inspected the River Welland. From Crowland to Spalding they found it very defective for want of dyking and cleaning, and from Spalding to the sea almost silted up because there had not been enough fresh water to scour out the channel. It was so bad that they had to put their boats into carts until they reached Fosdyke, where great ships lay at anchor.

In 1638 Sir William and Sir Antony Ayloff, with others, undertook the draining of these fens. They cleaned out the Welland and deepened its outfall, cleared drains, erected sluices and made partition dykes. The drainage adventurers had undertaken to make the navigable river 40ft broad and 6ft deep from Fosdyke to Deeping. This vast undertaking took a number of years to complete, but by 1642 they had widened and deepened the Welland from Waldron Hall to Spalding and thence to the sea. In 1634, during these improvements to the river, the old Roman stone bridge that had for 1,400 years been known as the Great Bridge of Spalding was taken down and a wooden structure erected in its place on the site of the present High Bridge. The old Roman stone bridge consisted of four arches but the navigation passed only through the centre two, the end arches having two towpaths underneath them. To make it safe and serviceable would have been expensive, and as the arches were too narrow to allow for a free passage of large barges it was deemed more expedient to pull it down. The wooden structure that replaced it was intended only as a temporary structure until they had sufficient funds to build a more substantial one, but the Civil War prevented this and the 'temporary' construction served its purpose for 200 years.

After the River Welland was deepened and widened by the drainage adventurers, shipping on the river increased enormously. Spalding was a sub-port to Boston and under that town's jurisdiction, a fact that was somewhat resented by the inhabitants of Spalding, especially in the light of this increased prosperity. They thought they would like to be a free port and manage their own affairs, so in 1695 the merchant traders and the principal inhabitants and others of Stamford and Holbeach petitioned to achieve this. Unfortunately the affair was dropped for want of a proper spirit to carry it forward. The book of rates at the custom house called Spalding a member of the Port of Boston and it was always styled 'Port of Spalding a Boston'. There was no custom house here, although there was a customer, a comptroller, etc.; the former had a silver seal of office by which Spalding was denominated a port. The device on the seal was a portcullis, an ancient cognisance of the king's exchequer. The inscription around it was SIGIL. OFFICII PORT. SPALDING, over which was C.R. for Carolus Rex, to show that it was made a port in the reign of Charles I.

The exports consisted chiefly of oats, rapeseed, line oil, wool and hides. The imports were stone, slates, coal and timber, salt, sugar and other groceries, pitch, tar, resin, lead, glass and beeswax. There was at that time no high duty on French wines; along with sack and sweet Spanish wines they came by way of Lynn and were brought here in smaller craft. Arrack and rum were little known, and even brandy, chocolate and coffee were rare. Teas were consumed only in some families and were chiefly bohea and stewed. All the sea coal consumed in Stamford, the county of Rutland and the Deepings, together with all the goods that went there by water carriage, passed through Spalding up the Welland.

Belonging to the town there were about seventy barges and other craft, each able to carry anything between 10 and 60 tons. Besides these, there were others that frequently came in from different places on the coast. Vessels of greater burden came no nearer the town than a place called Boston Scalps, about 8 to 10 miles away, where the barges discharged and took in their cargoes.

The 9½-mile navigation beside the River Welland from Stamford to Deeping St James where it joined the river to flow to Spalding and so on to the Wash was completed sometime between 1664 and 1673, under an Act

A map showing
the Welland
from Peakirk,
Market Deeping,
with Crowland
to Spalding,
c. 1736.

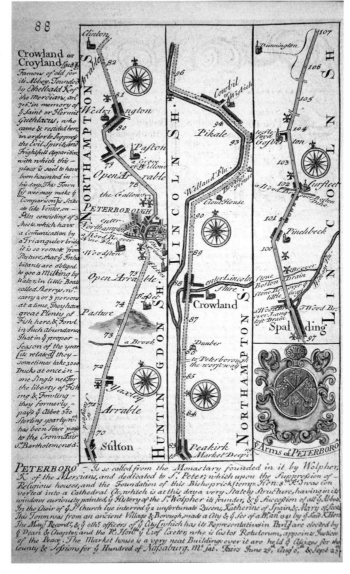

A map showing the Welland from Peakirk, Market Deeping, with Crowland to Spalding, c. 1736.

obtained by Stamford Corporation in 1620 confirming an Act of 1570 that had not been implemented. Cargoes carried on the canal included coal and groceries inwards and agricultural produce, malt, timber, stone and slates from Ketton and Collyweston outwards.

After the Welland was made navigable to Stamford, a flourishing malt trade developed in the town, and by 1700 malting and the malt trade were among its most thriving activities. Traffic on the canal from Stamford had to be transferred to lighters at Spalding and from them to seagoing vessels anchored in the Wash. Until the drainage of the fens in the seventeenth century, the river branched at Crowland. One portion flowed through Spalding as it does today. The other (known as the South Eau, the South Holland or Shire Drain) joined a branch of the Nene at No-man's-land-hirn and entered the sea by Cross Keys Wash. Dugdale, writing in the year 1660, tells us that this was the main channel and describes the other as flowing 'in a most slow course to Spalding and Surfleet', yet in 1878 this branch is described as a mere ditch and the main course through Spalding as 'a fine stream'.

Eighteenth Century

Captain John Perry was appointed engineer to the adventurers of Deeping Fen in 1730. The general idea of his scheme was to use scours to deepen the outfall by holding up the water and letting off the scours to grind out the silt and sand, and to make sluices across the Welland in several places. He further proposed deepening the River Welland and making it wider from the locks and sluices through the town of Spalding to Fosdyke and making two reservoirs, one at Cowbit Wash and another in the marshes opposite the Old Vernatts Outfall at Cowhirn. In 1730 he began his work with the construction of the great sluice next to Cowbit Wash at Locks Mill. When the doors were closed they held up the water in Cowbit Wash and when the water was released the outfall was ground and scoured out, carrying away the silt at the bottom of the river. However, it was soon discovered that the silt was not got rid of but only moved to settle a little lower downstream. Deepening the channel of the Welland from beyond Cowhirn to below Fosdyke was also attempted, a great number of workmen being employed to dig and barrow out the sand and silt. Captain Perry applied to the adventurers for leave to hold up the freshwaters but was refused, and in consequence this attempt proved ineffectual, for the tides filled up the channel almost as fast as the silt was taken out.

Although most of the drainage was of the fens, there were also many acres of coastal marshland reclaimed. During the Napoleonic Wars (1793–1815), 4,595 acres of marshland were embanked south of the River Welland in Spalding, Moulton, Whaplode, Holbeach and Gedney. In 1637, Sir Cornelius Vermuyden (1595–1683), the Dutch drainage engineer, had drained the Bedford Level and embanked the east side of the river to protect the North

Level from floods. The South Holland Drain began to be dug in the year 1794. In the same year a new cut was made from the reservoir to Fosdyke but the river continued to silt up owing to its defective outfall.

Nineteenth Century

The Welland runs through the east and a very ancient drain called the Westlode through the west side of the town, the latter forming communication with the river at the north end of it, whilst a branch of the drain formerly passed under the bed of the Welland and formed a junction with another drain[1] on the east side of that river, but which junction has lately been disannulled.

From the circumstances of these waters passing through the midst of the town and it being encompassed with almost innumerable drains and canals, it has frequently been compared by strangers to a Dutch town, and considering it is thus situated in the midst of the fens it is, upon the whole, a rather neater town than might be expected, but yet there is much room for amendment in this respect.

The Welland is navigable for barges and smaller craft through the centre of the town where there are several good quays and spacious storehouses on its banks. Spalding by this means has long enjoyed a good carrying and coasting trade …

In 1815 the neap tides did not reach Spalding. This state of things continued until, in the year 1835, the water was only a few inches deep …[2] Mr. James Walker C.E. thereupon devised and Mr. Beasley carried out the most admirable plan for improving the river by facine [sic] training.[3] Mr. Wheeler,

---

1 Lords Drain flowed past Fulney Church and Fulney Hall, then towards Weston, passing near Wool Hall, then to the east of Wykeham and on to its outfall into the Welland near Wragg Marsh Farm.

2 This must be an exaggeration, as shipping records show that in 1829, 250 vessels came in with a tonnage of 12,523; this increased by 1835 to 465 vessels in with a tonnage of 23,387.

3 Fascine work is described thus by Wheeler: 'Barrier walls or banks made of thorn faggots about six feet long and three feet girt, which are laid in the water in courses varying in width in proportion to the depth; and as each course, which is weighted with clay, sinks others are laid on till the bank is raised to about half-tide level. The branches of the thorns interlaced with one another, and the silt brought up by the tides rapidly deposits amongst and at the back of this facine [sic] work, and thus a solid embankment is formed, of sufficient strength and tenacity to withstand the strongest tidal current.'

writing on the subject, says that it was found to be so simple and inexpensive as compared with other methods, and at the same time so effective, that it has since been used in all similar works in the estuary.

In 1838 the temporary wooden town bridge erected in 1634 was at last taken down and replaced with the single-arch stone bridge that is still in place today. (E.H. Gooch, *The History of Spalding*, 1940)

There was a wooden footbridge upstream, known as Dinham's Bridge, which linked London Road to Cowbit Road. This bridge was replaced by a cast-iron suspension bridge in 1837. This being the year of Queen Victoria's accession to the throne it was named Victoria Bridge. This bridge fell down

The three-arched wooden town bridge dates from 1634. (H. Burgess, Spalding Gentlemen's Society collection)

A view of High Bridge from the River Welland in around 1900. (F. Parkinson, Spalding Gentlemen's Society collection)

Dinham's
Bridge.

Victoria Bridge
around 1900,
before it was
replaced by the
present one.
(F. Parkinson,
Spalding
Gentlemen's
Society collection)

on a stormy night in 1845 when the tide was high and the river was full of boats. It is thought that one of them ran against the bridge and broke the stays. It was re-erected before being replaced in 1868; the new bridge in turn was later replaced by the present structure.

The other footbridge downstream was known as Chain Bridge because it was swung on chains and opened to allow ships to pass through. This was briefly replaced by a temporary wooden one, and it was finally replaced by a swinging bridge in 1844, which was eventually demolished in June 1968. This bridge was named the Albert Bridge after Queen Victoria's consort, Prince Albert.

The old Chain Bridge in 1828, with its drawbridge sections open. (H. Burgess, Spalding Gentlemen's Society collection)

Fen lighters on the River Welland opposite Ayscoughfee Hall, in a postcard postmarked 1908.

The navigation was maintained in good order for the rest of the century as far as the town for sailing vessels and to the middle of the twentieth century for barges towed by a tugboat. The navigation to Stamford was open up until April 1863, when it became impossible for boats (fen lighters) to navigate due to the locks being in need of repair. Fen lighters were of a primitive form – big, open boats and slab-sided, with a hard chine, which had evolved to carry the maximum tonnage on the shallowest draught. The fen lighters were loaded with goods from Spalding and towed two or more at a time by horses, which were led along a towpath. Along the navigation from Stamford to East Deeping there were twelve locks 60ft long and 12ft wide.

Fen lighters upstream of the Victoria Bridge.

A lighter with the square sail is towed upriver by a horse. (H. Burgess, Spalding Gentlemen's Society collection)

Extracts From Writings on Spalding

In 1696, near the River Welland at Spalding, at the depth of about ten feet, there were found jetties to keep up the old river bank, and at the head of a tunnel that emptied the land water into the old river and about twenty or thirty yard's [sic] distance from the present river there were dug up at about the same depth several old boats, which showed that anciently the river was either much wider than it is now or ran in another place, or both. (E.H. Gooch, *A History of Spalding*, 1940)

Spalding, a Market Town of note, encompassed on every side with Rivers and Canals, yet neater than can reasonably be expected in a place that stands in the midst of Rivers and Lakes; for not only the River Welland washes the borders of it, but Boston and Langtoft Drains centre almost on it. The River Welland is navigable to this Town, and there are several Vessels and Barges belonging to this Port, though it be but small. (Thomas Cox, 1700)

Spalding. It is an ancient and well-built town and is a mile in length upon the road; but is in a low situation and enclosed with rivulets drains and a navigable river; which causes it to be a place of good trade, having several vessels and barges belonging to it. (*A Dictionary of the World*, 1772)

From Boston we came on through the fen country to Spalding, which is another sea port in the level, but standing far within the land on the River Welland. There is a bridge over the Welland, and vessels of about fifty or sixty ton may come up to the town, and that is sufficient for the trade of Spalding which is chiefly in corn and coal.

The town of Spalding is not large but pretty well built and well inhabited; but for the healthiness or pleasantness of it, I have no more to say than this that I was very glad when I got out of it, and out of the rest of the fen country; for 'tis a horrid air for a stranger to breathe in.

The history of the draining those fens, by a set of gentlemen called the Adventurers, the several laws for securing and preserving the banks and dividing the lands; how they were by the extraordinary conflux of waters from all the inland counties of England frequently overflowed, and sometimes lay under water most part of the year; how all the water in this part of England, which does not run into the Thames, the Trent, or the Severn, falls together into these low grounds, and empty themselves into the sea by those drains as thro' a sink; and how by the skill of these Adventurers, and, at a prodigious expense they have cut new channels, and even whole rivers, with particular drains from one river to another, to carry off the great flux of waters, when floods or freshes come down either on one side or on the other; and how notwithstanding all that hands could do, or art contrive, yet sometimes the waters do still prevail the banks break, and the whole levels are overflowed together.

We must not pass by Crowland; here there is one thing that is curious indeed, and very remarkable, and which is not to be seen in any other place in Britain, if be in Europe; namely a triangular bridge. The case is this; The River Welland and another river, or rather a branch from the River Nene, join together just at Crowland, and the bridge being fixed at the very point where they join, stands upon a centre in the middle of the united waters, and then parting into two bridges, lands you one to the right upon Thorney, and one to the left upon Holland. (Daniel Defoe, *A Tour Through the Whole Island of Great Britain*, Letter 7, Part 2: East Midlands, 1724–27)

All the corn grown in the interior parts of this country is brought up for the use of the inhabitants, and the surplus is sent to London in vessels belonging to Boston etc.

From Stamford and Deeping they send down Gangs of Lighters to be loaded with Coals for the supply of those parts of the country and a large district in the neighbourhood of Stamford. With the Coals they also carry up all the Grocery Goods brought hither from London, also Fir Timber, deals, pitch, Tar and other commodities imported from Boston, Lynn, Hull and Lincoln which are brought hither from those parts either by their own vessels or the Spalding Barges.

The Stamford Boats bring down from the High Country vast quantities of Flour, which being of a superior quality has a sale all over the Low Country, also Malt for which they are famous at Stamford, a great quantity of Limestone for the supplies of the Limekilns here, with paving stones and free Stone for Buildings, and Clapboards.

There are several annual fairs at Deeping for the sale of Wood and Timber. There are people who buy falls of Oak Timber and bring them down to these fairs, and others who make good Gates, trays, etc. and timber sawn into planks and scantlings fitted for the carpenters and wheelwrights. These are purchased by persons who want and those who deal in these articles.

Also large quantities of posts used for fencing in the marshes. All these commodities are sent down in the Welland and distributed all over the country. The boats coming for the coals, when the tide serves they are hauled by Horses down the river towards the Ships lying in Boston Scalp and receive the Coals immediately from out of the North Country Ships. At other times they are delivered by the Ships into Spalding Barges and then loaded in the Merchant Coal Yards from whence they can at all times be put on board the boats and sent upwards.

The River Glen unites with the Welland about four miles below Spalding. The boats on the Glen carry Coals etc. up to Bourne and bring Timber etc. from thence to Spalding. From this sketch of the internal trade up and down the Welland it is seen that the Boatmen have generally freight both upwards and downwards and thereby maintain their Gangs in a pretty constant course of trade when the river is of sufficient depth of water. (Notes from Thomas Hawkes's papers, written in 1792 for a directory of Spalding. Spalding Gentlemen's Society)

The Abbey was built in the year 1051, in the year 1286 the sea bank broke, and the waves came so strong that it washed down part of the Abbey wall, and to raise the money to repair the damage, the abbot laid a tax upon wool and flax in the parishes of Spalding, Pinchbeck, and Moulton.

In the year 1744, the River Welland was widened, and a beautiful row of Ash trees on each side of the river was taken down nearly to the High Bridge from the locks. The said locks were constructed under the superintendence of

Fosdyke Bridge in a drawing by G.W. Bailey dated 1906. (Spalding Gentlemen's Society collection)

Capt. John Perry, and he puddled the banks from the locks to the Three Doors Turn. The said doors were put down to run the water into the Westlode to ease the Wash. In the year 1813, the locks were taken up and the materials sold.

Near Spalding, in the course of the Welland to Deeping, is a place called Waldram Hall, from whence to Crowland was anciently a ferry, as this was at that time the only mode of travelling from this neighbourhood to that place, an idea may be found of the then state of that part of the country …

Opposite the Welland Inn, on the other side of the Welland stood a Boatwright's shop, kept by Mr Thomas Goodwin, who carried on an extensive trade in small craft, in the year 1805. It was removed by his son Richard to Marsh Road, later occupied by Mr Richardson, shipbuilder, 1848. Fosdyke Bridge was begun in 1814, and finished in 1814.[1]

The old crane at the bottom of Herring Lane, was put up by Mr Presgrave, who came from Bourne to reside as a merchant in the year 1795, there not being one before that time, they used to land the goods from the boats and barges in the coal yard opposite the Steam Mill public house in Double Street, kept by John Lamb, and years before that time by Mr Ray, coal merchant for up to three hundred years.

At Cowhirn, a short distance from Spalding, there was a noted ferry across the river Welland from Surfleet to Holbeach, for Scotch beast, which regularly came that way. There was a public house, the sign of the cow's horn, in the year 1763, kept by Mr Francis Frisby, grandfather to Mr William Hames, rope maker of Spalding.

In 1817 and the following years the River Westlode was enclosed in a brick tunnel of about 840 yards in an attempt to create a sewage and drainage system with its outlet into the River Welland. (Old Robin Harmstone, *Notices of Remarkable Events and Curious Facts with Various and Interesting Scraps Connected with the History and Antiquities of Spalding*, 1848)

Spalding, Lincolnshire, on the river Welland, 14 miles SW. of Boston, 12,070 ac., pop, 9260. Spalding is an important railway centre, while the river has been made navigable to the town for vessels of from 50 to 70 tons.

---

1   An Act of Parliament for the erection of a good and substantial bridge was granted in 1794 but funds were not available. A later Act in 1811 obtained Royal assent and funds were raised by several persons including Sir Joseph Banks. It was begun in 1812 and finished in 1815 built of whole trees of English Oak fully 18in diameter, and the centre had a double drawbridge for the passage of high-masted vessels. Previously there was a road across the Wash at this point at low water at Fosdyke and this was the only way for travellers to cross the Welland until the bridge was built.

It is situated in a rich agricultural district, and has a large trade, by river and by rail, in corn, wool, coal, and timber. It has also flour, bone, and saw mills, breweries, and coach works. There are remains of a priory of 1501, a fine old church (restored 1860), a grammar school, a corn exchange, and a spacious market place. (John Bartholomew, *Gazetteer of the British Isles*, 1887)

Spalding is a seaport town, a member of the port of Boston. In 1837 the river traffic was in full swing, the now decayed Pigeon End was the flourishing quarter of the town, populated by sailors and their families. The river was navigable for some distance beyond Stamford, and was the highway of communication for coals, agricultural produce, and all kinds of heavy goods, to all places near its course. The favourite promenade of the inhabitants at the time of high water was along the river side, from High Bridge to the Mill in the Marsh, the channel being crowded with craft of all sizes, from 20 to 150 tons burden. A Customs Officer kept diligent look out for all dutiable goods – (rather a numerous list at this period) – while the Harbourmaster had sometimes a difficult task in keeping order amongst the vessels and confining them to their proper positions. The language of Babel was fitly represented at high tides, embellished with many expletives in use amongst the sailor fraternity which are more forcible than polite. Some remains of the former traffic continue in the few granaries still existing in Double Street and High Street, but at that period those streets were continuous lines of those buildings. Wharves with powerful cranes were planted at the end of Herring Lane, and between the Albert Bridge and the Gasworks, and several firms throve in the now extinct business of wharfinger.

The river was spanned by three wooden bridges, the High Bridge, which was replaced by the present substantial stone structure, the year after the coronation; the Chain Bridge, which after successive conflicts with vessel masts, was finally worsted in the struggle, and replaced by the present Albert Bridge and the Dinham's Bridge, which afterwards gave place to an elegant iron structure, and this in turn to the present useful, if not ornamental, Victoria Bridge. (George Francis Barrell Esq., *Spalding Free Press* Diamond Jubilee Souvenir, 29 June 1897)

Welland Navigation By-laws

This is a copy of the by-laws drawn up by the trustees of the River Welland as an instruction to all persons using the navigation between the High Bridge and the outfall into the Wash in 1834:

At the annual meeting of the Trustees acting in the execution of an Act of Parliament passed in the fifth year of the reign of his late Majesty King George the Fourth, entitled 'An Act for explaining, amending, & rendering more effectual an Act of his late Majesty for improving the outfall of the River Welland in the County of Lincoln' Held at the Town Hall Spalding, in the County of Lincoln on Monday the 21st of April 1834, due notice having been given as required by the said Act, by advertisement in the *Lincoln Rutland and Stamford Mercury*; Present

Sir John Trollope Bart   Rev Dr Moore   Henry Hawkes jnr Esq
Mr Carter   Mr Parr   Mr Goodale   Mr Calthrop   Mr Harvey

It is now hereby resolved and ordained by us the said Trustees, by virtue & in exercise of the power given to us by the said recited Act, that the following Byelaws, orders, & constitutions, for the purpose of preserving, using or well governing the works of navigation vested in us, or placed under our direction & care, by the said recited Act, shall be & the same are hereby ordained & established to be observed by all persons interested therein or frequenting or trading on the River Welland, under pain of fines and forfeitures for the breach thereof or any of them hereinafter specified and set forth.

We constitute and appoint Mr Samuel Capps to be the superintendent or controller of the navigation of the said river Welland, for all the purpose of these by-laws and orders, under the name or title of Harbour Master.

The Captain or Master of light or unladen craft navigating the said river shall give way to loaded vessels coming up or going down the river.

The Captain or Master of any vessel coming up or going down with the tide or current shall not do any act to prevent loaded vessels, which are hauling against current keeping their lines.

That no Captain or Master of a vessel shall, under any pretence whatever, attempt to pass another vessel without sufficient water.

That no Captain or Master shall place his vessel between the piers of the Chain or Drawbridge, or in a direct line therewith, either above or below, unless there be sufficient depth of water to insure the passing of his vessel, such depth of water to be ascertained by a table or index, which shall be forthwith placed at the bridge and marked with a scale of feet and inches to denote the depth of water.

That every Captain or Master not taking in or discharging his cargo shall moor his vessel on the south side of the river, shall use all practical means to facilitate the navigation by other vessels, and shall not wilfully obstruct or do any act to hinder the passage and mooring of any other vessel.

That no vessel drawing more than seven feet, be permitted to come higher up the river than Baileys Gate, that drawing more than six feet of water higher up than the Pigeon Granary, while drawing more than five feet and a half of water higher up than the Albion Granary, & while drawing more than five feet of water higher up than High Bridge. Nevertheless this regulation shall be subject to such temporary alteration from time to time as in the judgement of the Harbour Master shall be fit & expedient, in consequence of any increased depth of the channel of high tides or floods, of which alteration the Harbour Master shall give notice in writing to be left with the Custom House Officer for the time being.

That no vessel be loaded as to draw or require a greater depth of water than next mentioned, within the following stations viz:- between the High Bridge & Albion Granary five feet, between the Albion Granary & Pigeon Granary Five & a half, & between the Pigeon Granary & Baileys Gate six feet, unless with leave of the Harbour Master.

That no Captain or Master of a vessel shall Quit his ship during tide time, without leaving on board a competent & responsible man to do what is needful in compliance with these orders & if any vessel be left without some competent man on board, the Harbour Master shall place one there & the expense shall be paid by the Captain or Master of the vessel to the Harbour Master on demand over & beyond the fine or penalty.

That the Pilot who for the time being shall have the charge of any vessel, & shall violate any of these orders & regulations, shall be liable to the penalty attached to the offence.

That the Captain or Master & crew of any vessel do obey & conform to all the orders of the Harbour Master, so far as the same be in the furtherance of & conformable with the spirit & intent of the foregoing regulations.

That the fine, penalty, & forfeiture for a breach or wilful violation of any & each & every of the foregoing orders & regulations, be not less than the sum of Ten shillings, nor more than the sum of Five pounds, at the discretion of the Justices of the Peace before whom the commission of the offence shall be proved.

By Order

Chas. Bonner, Clerk to the said Trustees.

Rivers and Drains Flowing into the Welland

The Westlode had existed since Roman times and flowed from its junction with the River Glen at Pinchbeck Bars along a drain alongside Dozens Bank to Pode Hole, then along what is now Bourne Road, Winsover Road, New Road and Westlode Street, to enter the Welland between Double Street and Albion Street, where there were sluice doors to hold up the water for navigation.

Farmers conveyed their cattle and other produce to the market in Spalding by barges along this navigation. When the tide was high the barges would go through the sluice and transfer goods onto the seagoing vessels in the Welland to be sent on to other ports along the east coast, and load other cargo brought in on those ships for the return journey. On John Grundy's 1732 map of Spalding there appears to be a small dock or turning area inside the sluice gates on the Albion Street side. There were bridges over the Westlode: an old Roman one between Double Street and Albion Street, footbridges opposite Pinchbeck Road and the White Swan Inn in New Road, a wagon bridge to Boston at the bottom of Red Lion Street and another bridge opposite St Thomas's Road known as Betty Codlin's bridge.

There was also a culvert draining water from the Westlode under the bed of the Welland near the Chain Bridge into the Lord's Drain. This was taken up in 1917–18, and then when the steam pumps were erected at Pode Hole in 1824 the navigation of the Westlode to the Glen was no longer possible so it was arched over for 840 yards from near the White Swan to the Welland for drainage of sewage and rainwater, and the rest was filled in with silt taken from the Welland.

The River Glen enters the Welland at Surfleet Reservoir, where there are sluice doors that could be opened for navigation when the water was of an equal level. Goods could be loaded from the seagoing ships onto barges or lighters of around 15 tons burden to be taken upstream, and goods brought downstream were loaded onto these ships to be taken away. The Glen was only really navigable up to a few miles above Tongue End, although it may have been possible to go as far as Greatford at one time as there are the remains of some moorings at Greatford Hall.

Some boats for goods and passengers left from Bourne every Tuesday, market day, but this service was unreliable as there would sometimes be either too little or too much water. This situation was improved by the installation of self-acting doors at Tongue End at the junction with the Bourne Eau.

The River Welland at Surfleet Seas End, the entrance to the River Glen.

Pode Hole, near Spalding   Valentines Series   28489

Lighters and a steam tug near to Pode Hole pumping station. (Spalding Gentlemen's Society collection)

Water sports at Surfleet Reservoir: a swimming race starting from a lighter. (Spalding Gentlemen's Society collection)

The opening of the railway line from Spalding to Bourne in 1866 made this navigation redundant, and a sluice at Tongue End later shut off the Bourne Eau. At the Surfleet railway station next to the River Glen there was a basin where goods were interchanged from the Spalding to Boston railway line, and there were a few barges still using the last mile or more upriver until the mid-1920s.

The Glen is still navigable for a few miles above the Surfleet Reservoir for small pleasure boats, and a number of other larger ones are kept on moorings in the outfall of the river near the 'Ship Inn' and venture down to the Wash for pleasure trips (locally known as 'going down below') when the tides allow. I had the pleasure of a trip once with friends belonging to the Welland Yacht Club, during which we landed on the Roger Sand to collect cockles.

3

TYPES OF VESSEL USING THE PORT OF SPALDING

The Humber Keel

The Humber keel was a descendant of the trading vessels that carried cargo up and down the coast for many years before it. With only a single mast and a large square sail, not unlike the sails on Roman merchant ships, Viking longships and medieval vessels, it was not able to sail into the wind, so it was more suitable for carrying cargo on the inland rivers and canals. The smaller barges and lighters that carried cargo up the River Welland would have been rigged in the same way and used the sail when they had a following wind, otherwise they had to be towed inland by horse.

The Humber Sloop

Many of the early vessels would have been Humber sloops. These were around 68ft long with a beam of 16ft and a draft of 8ft. They would carry 130 tons or more of cargo. With heavily built clincher or carvel hulls constructed in timber, sloops carried a gaff and boom rig with triangular main- and headsails. Early sloops carried a bowsprit with the jib set on a stay, plus a flying jib hanked to the topmast stay. The bulwarks on this type are raised and the cargo hatch is divided into two: a small one forward of the mast and a long large one aft of it. The mast was stepped above the deck in a very strong wooden lutchet.

The sloops and other vessels from Spalding traded mainly along the coast from the Wash ports to the North Sea ports of Newcastle, Sunderland, Middlesbrough, Hartlepool, Stockton and Seaham, and to the Humber

Humber keels with square sails set, 1899. (Lincolnshire Library Service, postcard set No. 3, 1978)

A basic clincher-built sloop with leeboards, a loose-footed gaff mainsail and a jib.

ports of Hull, Selby, Keadby, and Goole, carrying produce from Lincolnshire and returning with coals and other goods, and also South to Lynn, Ipswich, London and as far as Plymouth on the South Coast with produce including grain and oak timber. Accommodation was in a skipper's cabin under the afterdeck and a crew cabin under the foredeck.

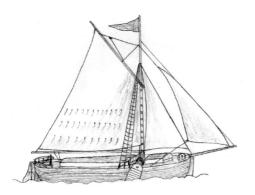

A clincher-built sloop with a bowsprit, jib and flying jib.

A Humber sloop, flying jib furled and with a cog boat astern, enters Hull Dock. Later versions, like this one built of steel, were simpler-looking vessels with more powerful mechanical equipment for handling the heavier spars and greater loads. (From a glass plate by William Jackson)

A clincher-built sloop with a gaff topsail and two flying jibs.

A billy-boy cutter with a loose-footed mainsail, two foresails and square topsails.

The Billy-boy Cutter, Ketch and Schooner

The name 'billy-boy' was derived from the earlier square-rigged vessels known as 'bilanders' (from Dutch meaning 'by lander') that sailed up and down the coast keeping in sight of land. A bilander was a small European merchant ship with two masts, used in the Netherlands for coast and canal traffic and occasionally seen in the North Sea but more frequently to be seen in the Mediterranean. The mainmast was lateen-rigged with a trapezoidal mainsail, but the foremast carried the conventional square sail and square topsail. They rarely reached a size of more than 100 tons.

The smallest of the billy-boy class were cutter rigged. These were typical of the small traders of the first half of the nineteenth century. With the addition of a second headsail and a square topsail, they carried more sail than the sloop. To get the gaff aloft and the topsail set they needed a crew of three. The billy-boy cutters were clincher built with a conventional keel, but they required leeboards to make working to windward effective. Smaller versions were 45ft in length, drawing 7ft, and loaded only 40 tons. They were well known in the Wash ports and traded along the east coast regularly, making profitable voyages. Some of these would have had owners and Masters living in Spalding.

The billy-boy ketches and schooners were the seagoing development of the Humber sloop and the billy-boy cutter. Some had started life as sloops and had then been lengthened and re-rigged as ketches or schooners.

The length overall was up to 90ft, with a beam of 18ft. They had a long main hatch, and the masts were set in substantial wooden tabernacles carried down to the keelson. A heavy cargo winch abaft the mainmast was also used for setting sail.

A watercolour painting of a ketch-rigged billy-boy with a square topsail, a small topgallant sail and three headsails.

A schooner rigged
billy-boy, from a painting
by Edward Gentle.

A seagoing sloop and a
smaller vessel wait for
the tide downriver from
Spalding, around 1900.
(F. Parkinson, Spalding
Gentlemen's Society
collection)

All except the largest billy-boys had a simple barrel windlass in the bow, worked by handspikes. The boat was carried on the main hatch. The hulls of the larger billy-boys were the same shape as their cutter-rigged predecessors and almost always clincher built up to the end of the nineteenth century – the largest vessels of this construction in north-west Europe.

The ketches had a large mainmast with gaff and boom, a main gaff topsail, a smaller mizzenmast with a gaff and boom, a square topsail, a small topgallant sail and two or three headsails.

A schooner-rigged billy-boy had two masts of the same height. The forward foremast had a smaller gaff and boom sail, while the larger rear mast was the mainmast and had a larger gaff and boom sail. Like the ketch, the schooner also carried a fore gaff topsail, a main gaff topsail, a square topsail on the foremast and a small topgallant sail.

4

FAMILY HISTORY

Great-Great-Grandfather Matthew Southwell Vine, Master Mariner

The first record of my ancestor is his marriage certificate. He was married on 25 May 1842 to Hannah Buttler. Matthew's father John Vine was a miller, but Hannah was the daughter of Henry Buttler, who was also a mariner. One of the witnesses to the marriage was George Levesley, a mariner and captain of Joseph Henry Bugg's yacht. Matthew and Hannah had a daughter Hannah Susan in 1843 and a son John Henry (perhaps named after his grandfathers) in 1854.

In 'Shipping News' in the *Lincoln, Rutland & Stamford Mercury* for the period to 9 April 1843 I find him for the first time as a captain on the *Ancholm*, which had arrived from Goole with 'goods, coal, deals etc.'. On 19 April 1843 he sailed again on the *Ancholm* to Goole with wheat grain and other goods.

In 'Spalding Ship News' in the *Spalding Free Press* for the period to 3 May 1848 he was captain of the *Ellen* and sailed to Sunderland with 'oak timber etc.'.

I find him next in 1850 on a page of a ledger account of work and materials made out to him by blacksmith Edward Fisher at the blacksmith's shop near the Chain Bridge, later the premises of the Dodd family. Unfortunately the name of the vessel is not recorded on this page.

The next entry for Matthew Southwell Vine in the blacksmith's ledger is in January 1862 and names the *Breeze*. There are also pages for 1863, 1864 and 1865 naming the *Breeze*.

In early May 1851 he again sailed to Sunderland on the *Ellen* and returned from Stockton on 26 May with coals. Then I found a Captain

Vine in a list of arrivals from Middlesbrough with coals on the *Thomas and Jane* on 20 June 1851, but in July a Captain Vine sailed on the *Ellen* again to the north.

According to 'Spalding Ship News' to 10 August 1857, he sailed on the *Breeze* to the North and Humber with others in ballast.

In the census of 1861 I find Matthew as Master of the sloop *Breeze*, registered at Boston, 54 tons burden. The rest of the crew consisted of a mate, John Enderby; a seaman, Robert Geant; and boy, John Vine (great-grandfather John Henry). Although the vessel is recorded at this time as a sloop, the picture I have, which was taken later, shows it rigged as a billy-boy ketch. An entry in the *Boston Ships Register* on 22 October 1870 shows that it was re-registered after being altered from a sloop to a ketch.

In 1861 and 1862 there are entries for the schooner *Samuel Barnard*, captained by Joseph Vine, Matthew's younger brother and my great-great--great-uncle. I found the *Samuel Barnard* in the 1861 census registered at Boston, 60 tons burden, and 'at sea' at the time of the census. The rest of the crew comprised the mate, John Worly; a seaman, Thomas Dunn; and a boy, John Chatterton. John Chatterton was the nephew of Matthew and Joseph, the son of their sister Louisa Chatterton (*née* Vine), who was a witness at Matthew's wedding.

In *White's Directory* of 1856 he is listed under 'Mariners, Sloop and Boat Masters' as Vine, Matthew, Willow Row.

A postcard, featuring the *Breeze* on the River Welland.

Matthew Southwell Vine's Masters Certificate of Service.

In the *Post Office Directory* of 1868 he is listed as Vine, Matthew, beer retailer, coal merchant and shipowner, Commercial Road.

In *White's Directory* of Spalding of 1872 he is listed as Vine, Matthew, shipowner, No. 27 Willow Row Walk. In the same 1872 directory his son John Henry is listed as master mariner, No. 36 High Street.

I have been unable to find Matthew again in any other censuses or directories.

He died on 10 June 1878 and is buried in plot G in Spalding cemetery, which is on the right-hand side about 60 yards from the entrance. His will was proved by Hannah Vine on 4 July 1878; his personal estate was under £200.

In a *Spalding Free Press* article dated 25 November 1919, Captain John Turner is quoted as saying: 'I can remember the chief captains of the old days; Sam Culpin, Gosterlow, Hayes, Royce, Chester, Joe Vine, Matthew Vine, and John and Joseph Atkin.'

Joseph Vine, Master Mariner

Joseph Vine was born in 1825 and married Mary Woods in 1849. His children were Anne Maria (b. 1851), Eliza Jane (b. 1853, d. 1865), John Joseph (b. 1856, d. 1887) and Rebecca Alice (b. 1860, d. 1888).

In the 1861 census he is master of the *Samuel Barnard*, 60 tons burden, registered at Boston, and at sea at the time of the census. In an 1862 entry in the ledger of the blacksmith Edward Fisher, he is still master of the schooner *Samuel Barnard*

In 1881 Joseph is master of the *Leo XIII*, 77 tons burden, registered at Newcastle, which was at Town Quay, Southampton, at the time of the census. Crew members were the mate, William Hesory; seaman, Fredrick Luff; and seaman, George Golding.

In 1891 Joseph is with his sister and niece in Islington, London. His wife Mary was living at No. 43 Commercial Road, Spalding on her own.

Joseph died in 1895 aged 70, and his death was registered at Stepney London. Mary is still alive in the 1901 census, aged 75 and living with granddaughter Mary R. Vine, aged 27. The following is an extract from Joseph's will:

> To my wife Mary, Sailing vessels or shares in any such vessels be realized and such monies to my wife throughout her lifetime and on her decease to my four children divided equal, John Joseph, Anne Maria B., Rebecca Alice and Mary Louisa Vine.
>
> Witness, Margery Pratt and Joseph Brown Pratt, Schoolmasters, Spalding

Unfortunately three of these children died before him.

Joseph Vine's Master's Certificate of Service.

John Henry Vine, Master Mariner

John Henry was born 1854. He was master of the *Breeze* after Matthew. He is listed again in *Kelly's Directory* of 1885 as a master mariner. John Henry married Rebecca Ann Draper in June 1870. Rebecca was the daughter of Thomas Draper, who was also a shipowner, as well as landlord of the Ship Albion public house. This was the headquarters of the Spalding Shipwreck Society from when it was founded in 1844 until 1977. Thomas Draper was the president of the society in 1850. John Henry and Rebecca Ann had three sons and three daughters:

Florence Daisy, born 1872, married Julius Corderny and had a daughter Marjorie.

Eva King, born 1876, married Harry Leeson at Christchurch.

Thomas Henry, born 1878, married Elizabeth Nicholson of Louth.

Edith Ada, born 1880, married Herbert Seaton and had sons Ralph (my father) born 1907 and Thomas born 1909, and a daughter Edith Molly born 1911.

Roland, born 1882, lost his life in the First World War, on 15 October 1917 in 10th Battalion Essex Regiment, and is buried at Poelcapelle British cemetery.

George Harry, born 1884, married Annie Vine and had a son Harry in 1910. Harry Vine married but had no children and died in October 1996, the last descendant of Matthew Southwell Vine with the name Vine.

Great-grandfather John Henry Vine, master mariner, (1846–1923).

5

SOME OTHER SPALDING MARINERS

The Grassam Family

Seth Grassam was born in 1815 and married Sarah Hall in 1840. In 1861 he was recorded as an agriculture machinery maker living in Cross Street, Spalding. His oldest son William, born in 1845, succeeded him as owner of the business. He lived in Cross Street and had a foundry off the Crescent in Spalding. He died in February 1911.

William Henry Grassam (1845–1911).

Captain John Richard Grassam.

John Richard Grassam was born in 1848, the second son of Seth and Sarah Grassam. In February 1875 he gained his Board of Trade Certificate of Competency as Second Mate. In February 1877 he gained his Certificate as First Mate and in June 1878 his Certificate as Master Mariner. In 1882 he married Sarah Hannah Draper, a sister of Rebecca Ann, and so was brother-in-law to John Henry Vine.

John Richard received his Board of Trade Certificate of Competency as Master in the Merchant Service on 27 June 1878. His records show that he was on the *Tweed* in 1880. The *Tweed* had been built as a paddle-wheel frigate named *Punjaub* in the Mumbai dockyard and launched in 1857. Later bought by J. Willis in 1862 and converted to sail, it had some outstanding voyages. She was commanded by Capt. J.M. Whyte in 1880, who had been in command of the *Blackadder* previously. *Tweed* left London on 12 May and arrived in Sydney on 29 July (seventy-five days out). She then left Sydney on 1 October 1880 and arrived in London on 28 December (eighty-eight days out).

In 1881 John Richard received his first command, namely that of the barque *Laurel*, another of John Willis's ships. He held this position up to 1889, when he became the master of the clipper ship *Blackadder*.

Blackadder was one of the last clippers designed and intended for the lucrative China tea trade before that route finally succumbed to steamships in the late 1870s. Launched from the Greenwich yards of Maudsley, Sons & Field on 1 February 1870, it was built for John Willis of London, the

The *Tweed*, owned by John Willis & Son.

The barque *Laurel*, owned by John Willis & Son.

The clipper ship *Blackadder* was 970 tons in full sail.

owner of two of the most celebrated clippers of them all, namely *Tweed* and *Cutty Sark*. Sadly it could never match their prowess, although it proved a fast ship when skilfully handled and had luck on its side – advantages it lacked for most of its life. Registered at 970 tons gross (917 net), *Blackadder* measured 216ft 6in in length with a 35ft 2in beam and a 20ft 5in depth and was identical to its sister ship *Halloween*, which had been constructed alongside it from lines taken from the *Tweed*. Unfortunately, Maudsley, Sons & Field had made their name as engineers and had little experience actually building ships. Serious errors were made when fitting its masts, and her dismasting on its maiden voyage merely confirmed Willis's mistake in selecting that yard to build it. In fact, its first passage was a catalogue of mishaps, some of them near disasters, and *Blackadder* gained an immediate reputation as an unlucky ship. Eventually settling into a routine schedule, it turned in one near-record passage from Deal to Shanghai in ninety-five days during the north-east monsoon in 1872, but was dismasted again in 1873 and nearly wrecked twice in the same year.

Her later career on the Australian wool run under the command of John Richard Grassam was less accident-prone. Some notable passages were made and the *Blackadder* became the centre of interest in shipping circles both in London and Australia. Some of these passages are as follows: in 1890 from 27 November to 26 February it sailed from Brisbane to London in ninety-one days with a cargo of wool. In 1893 from 20 December to 30 March it sailed from Brisbane to London in 100 days, again with a cargo of wool. In 1894 from 20 October to 20 February it sailed from Brisbane to London in 123 days, again with a cargo of wool. In 1897 it sailed from Brisbane to London in seventy-nine days. Its best four-day run was accomplished in 1899 from Hobart to Port Chalmers, averaging about 300 miles a day. Other records show that for thirty-seven days this ship achieved an average of 240 miles a day.

Eventually sold to Norwegian owners in 1900 after Willis's death, it was lost on 5 November 1905 whilst en route from Barry, South Wales, to Bahia, Brazil, with a full cargo of coal.

Grassam's home address in 1899 was Albert Street, Spalding, but by 1911 he was living at No. 16 Bond Street, Clerkenwell, London, and recorded as a retired master mariner. He died aged 84 in January 1933 and his death was registered at Finsbury, London.

William Grassam, John Richard's brother, was married to Sarah Ann Smith and their second son, John George, also became a mariner.

John George Grassam gained his Certificate of Competency as Second Mate in the Merchant Service in June 1889, Certificate as First Mate in July 1891, Certificate as Master in June 1893 and Certificate as Extra Master of a Foreign-going Ship in the Merchant Service in December 1897. His record of merchant service shows him in command of the following list of vessels: 1894–97 *Adjutant*, 1898 *Helvingrove*, 1899 *Jetuan*, 1900 *Tern*, *Albatross* and *Merlin*, 1901 *Vesuvio*, 1902 *Merannio* and *Vesuvio*, and 1903 *Guillemot*. All of the vessels in this list have been marked with an '(s)', presumably indicating that they were steamships. He was a Royal Navy voluntary reserve lieutenant on the navy list in November 1903, and in 1911 he was a Board of Trade nautical surveyor living in Swansea, Glamorgan. He died on 4 January 1927 at Hyndland, Glasgow.

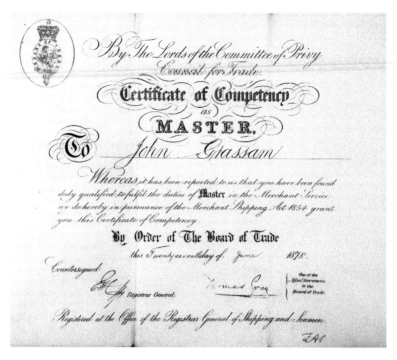

John Richard Grassam's Master's Certificate.

John George Grassam's Certificate of Competency as Extra Master.

Captain George Levesley.

Captain George Levesley was another master mariner; he was born in Spalding on 28 August 1821. His parents were William and Mary and he was baptised on 18 October 1831. His father's occupation is given as 'writer'.

There was another family living in Spalding at the same time who may be related, that of William Fredrick and Ann Levesley. In 1841 William Fredrick was a sailor with three children: John aged 9; George aged 5; and William aged 3.

Captain George had lived in Willow Row Walk and is listed as master of the *Breeze* in Edward Fisher's ledger in 1856.

In 1842 he had been a witness to the marriage of my great-great-grandfather Matthew Southwell Vine. He was known to be the skipper of Mr Joseph Henry Bugg's private yacht *Red Rover*, of 20 tons, in which the owner cruised around the coast of Great Britain and to the near continent.

Captain George Levesley.

This painting of the *Breeze*, dated 11 September 1856, shows the vessel as a cutter-rigged sloop, but it was altered to a ketch in 1870. (My thanks for permission to include this go to Mr Tony Levesley)

Mrs Turner in her 'Tales of the Sea' (in *A History of Spalding* by E.H. Gooch) tells of the yacht having a false bottom put in it to hide tobacco and spirits that could be bought cheaply on the Continent. On one homeward trip this was discovered by the custom officers and there was a hullabaloo about it. Bugg swore he knew nothing about it and that Captain Levesley was responsible, and so the captain was prosecuted and heavily fined. However, it was supposed that Mr Bugg indirectly paid it for him.

In a report in the *Lincolnshire Free Press* on 3 June 1856, George Levesley was recorded as the skipper of the *Red Rover* when it took part in the Royal Boston Yacht Club regatta. The respected representative for Boston, Mr Herbert Ingram, presented to the club a very handsome 50 guinea cup, leaving it to the members to dispose of it as they thought proper. They judiciously determined to throw it open for competition among the yachts belonging to the club, charging a 1s per ton entrance. The money this raised formed a second prize to be competed for by yachts under 5 tons burden. There were eight entries for the Ingram Cup and four for the smaller prize.

Unfortunately *Red Rover* was bringing up the rear in this race and its racing career was cut short by its running upon the Ants Sand, where it remained until the tide turned in the evening; but at the time it was so far astern as to have almost lost sight of the other yachts. They rounded the winning-buoy in the following order: *Waterwitch*, *Magic*, *Fairy* and *Kitten*.

The next regatta, in August 1857, attracted thirteen entries but was marred by the tragic loss of one of the smaller boats; the *Phantom* was sunk when a heavy sea struck it side-on. Of the crew of three fishermen, Webster, Cox and Royal, only Webster was saved. Although Cox was sighted in the water he disappeared from view, and he and Royal were presumed drowned.

In May 1861 Captain Levesley arrived at Fosdyke from Southampton with a new yacht belonging to Mr J.H. Bugg named *Sylph*. The registration certificate for *Red Rover* in the name of 'Henry Bugg' had been cancelled at the Port of London in December 1860, at which time it was presumably sold to another owner.

George Levesley married Isabella Priestley on 29 January 1846. They went on to have four sons: William (b. 1852), George (b. 1858), Frederic Henry (b. 1862) and James Henry (b. 1865). According to a local directory, 1885 he was still living at No. 22 Albert Street, but by 1889 he had moved to Mariner Ville in Willow Walk. His fourth son, James Levesley, was now living at No. 22 Albert Street. Both George and Isabella were listed as living with William (a widower) and his son George in Double Street in the 1891 census, and again in 1901.

The yachts start the race for the cup at Boston Regatta. (*London Illustrated News*, 14 June 1856)

Captain Levesley's Master's Certificate of Service.

George was an active member of the Spalding Shipwreck Society, possibly a founder member, and in 1903 was referred to as 'the grand old man of the Society'. He died in June 1914 at the age of 93.

In 1977 his grandson Mr Fred Oliver Levesley was vice president of the society.

The Turner Family

In an article in the *Spalding Free Press* on 25 November 1919, John Edward Turner tells us that his grandfather John Turner (1770–1833) took part in a voyage of discovery to the Pacific: 'Two ships were fitted out by the King in 1791 and sailed to the Pacific where they were engaged on survey work on the coast of Canada and the United States and elsewhere.' This voyage was with Commander George Vancouver on HMS *Discovery*. George Vancouver was born in King's Lynn on 22 June 1757 and at the age of 15 joined the navy as a midshipman and sailed with Captain James Cook during his second and third voyages. In 2nd Lt Peter Puget's log, John Turner, able seaman, is in the muster tables of His Majesty's Sloop *Discovery*, which were taken on 1 April 1791, the day the vessel left Falmouth. In the final muster

John Turner, born around 1771 in Lincolnshire.

tables, dated 3 November 1795, is the following entry: 'Entered 10th July 1791 place Cape of Good Hope born Lincolnshire; age 21; name Jn Turner AB. [Able Seaman].' The ship had now completed its voyage and was back in England. The *Discovery* went aground on the 6 August 1792 in Queen Charlotte Strait. In a ship's log following its refloating on a rising tide on Tuesday 7 August, there is the following entry: 'The lower yards topmast and topgallant masts were swayed up and the topgallant yards crossed. In swaying up the topgallant mast Jonathan Turner, seaman, fractured his right arm when the mast rope or top rope broke causing the mast to fall.' In the log of Midshipman John Sykes, the same incident is recorded but with the name John Turner. The arm remained weak for many months and he continued to do his duty as best he could. Sadly, whilst trying to deal with a heavy duty he fell overboard and had to be rescued. For this George Vancouver ordered him to be flogged. Another of the ship's logs records that on 19 March 1793 Turner was given twenty-four lashes for 'neglect of duty'.

In *A History of Spalding* by E.H. Gooch (1940), Mrs Turner (his grandson John's second wife) imparts that on his return from the expedition John was pressed into service with the Royal Navy and later served at the Battle of Trafalgar. John Turner was most likely the boatswain on HMS *Ajax* at Trafalgar; his service record commences on 4 July 1795 and includes service on the *Ajax*. On that same date, 4 July 1795, seventeen men were sent from the *Discovery*, which was travelling homeward in a convoy of twenty-four vessels, to the Dutch prize *Macassar* which sailed under the protection of a Royal Navy convoy to England. On 23 October 1795 George Vancouver sent a letter to the Admiralty and drew to their attention the unfairness of preventing the men's return to family and friends after an absence of nearly five years; their fate is unknown. However, given the coincidence of dates it is quite possible that John Turner was one of them.

On completion of his naval service he married Mary Turner and settled in Hull (Sculcoates). A son John was born and baptised on 13 May 1815 and a daughter Mary Frances was born and baptised on 6 April 1817, both at Sculcoates. The family moved to Spalding sometime before 1835. Mary died in Church Street, Spalding, in 1851.

His daughter Mary Frances married Samuel Capps Belcham in 1837. He was a pilot and was perhaps related to the Samuel Capps who was Harbour Master in 1834. Mary Frances died in Spalding in 1871.

His son John married Harriet Burdett on 22 January 1835 at Spalding. They had four children but only one son survived into adulthood. Another son, Burdett, died at Scarborough of smallpox on 20 May 1857 at the age of 15 years; despite his young age he was already described as a merchant seaman.

The surviving son, John Edward Turner (1839–1926), was christened on 20 September 1839. Following his father's death in 1844, his mother Harriet married Thomas Royce, another Spalding mariner, in 1849 and they had three children.

In an article published on 25 November 1919 in the *Lincolnshire Free Press*, John tells of his early sailing experiences:

> As a young man I sailed as far as the Baltic ports and the Mediterranean to Marseilles and also to Dunkirk. We took coals and brought home wheat, deals, and hemp. We made the voyage to Kronstadt in the Baltic and back in eight weeks. Kronstadt was a busy port on the mouth of the Neva, with the capital of Russia, St Petersburg, twelve miles above. We could see the spires of that city on a clear day. About that time they did away with serfdom in Russia.

A long-standing member of the Shipwreck Society, his stepfather Thomas Royce put John Edward in the society when he was about 20 years old.

Captain John Edward Turner. (Photograph supplied by his great-grandson Richard Walker)

He married Eliza Ann Ladd on 25 December 1862, when both bride and groom were aged 23, at St Mary and St Nicholas church, Spalding. However, within just a few weeks he was at sea again; according to 'shipping news' for the period to 10 January 1863 he sailed to Leith with a cargo of carrots and he continued to sail in and out of port regularly until 1868. On the 1871 census his boat the *Sarah* was at Snettisham Beach, Norfolk. In 1872 he was living at No. 6 Commercial Road, Spalding. In 1892 he was landlord with his wife Elizabeth Ann at the Angel Inn, Double Street, Spalding. By 1919 he was Harbour Master as well as landlord of the Angel Inn, Double Street. It was at this time that the article about him was published in the *Lincolnshire Free Press*.

The Royce Family

The Royce family was another local family that had many mariners and fishermen sailing out of the River Welland and elsewhere.

A Thomas Royce, born around 1770, and his wife Rebecca had sons John (b. 1791), William (b. 1799) and Joseph (b. 1803).

John Royce, a mariner born 1791, married Ann Bouice on 31 August 1813 at Frieston. He had a son Thomas (b. 9 December 1813) and daughters Ann (b. 1817), Eliza (b. 1821) and Martha Morris (b. 1826).

William Royce, a sailor, married Martha Ibbott on 16 July 1821. They had sons John (b. 10 July 1822), William (b. 2 July 1824) and Richard (b. 29 December 1826) and a daughter Martha (b. 1 December 1828). The mother Martha died and was buried on 3 December 1828, and her newborn daughter died and was buried on 18 January 1829. William married again on 11 June 1829 to Elizabeth Belton and had more children: Thomas (b. 1830), Jane (b. 1831), Rebecca (b. 1834), Edward (b. 1837), Joseph (b. 1840), Elizabeth (b. 1844) and Ann (b. 1847).

A Peter Royce was Master and part-owner of a clinker-built sloop *Bee*, of 45 tons burden and registered at Boston in 1828.

A John Royce was Master of the *Unity*, a carvel-built sloop, in 1832; Master and part-owner of *Friendship* in 1833; and also Master and part-owner of *Freedom* in 1833. All were registered at Boston.

On 15 August 1845 Thomas Royce, mariner, married Susannah Dixey; the groom's father was William, a fisherman.

On 8 July 1849, Thomas Royce (b. 1813) married Harriet Turner (widow of John Turner); the groom's father was John, a mariner. They had children William (b. 1850), Harriet (b. 1856) and Thomas (b. 1857). I have been told that one of these sons was mate on the clipper ship *Ariel*, which famously took part in the 'Great Tea Race' – in 1866 *Ariel* and *Taeping* raced from Foochow, China, to London with the first tea crop of the season. As William would have been only 16 and Thomas only 9 in 1866 it was probably at a later date that they joined the *Ariel* (but before 1872 when it was lost on a voyage to Sydney). The ship *Laurel*, a sloop rig of 35 tons burden, was later registered in Boston as owned by Mrs Harriet Royce. Its registration number was 5325 and it was built in Doncaster in 1838.

John Royce, a mariner born in Spalding, married Gwynn Williams on 20 February 1845. On the 1851 census he was described as aged 30 and was living at Waterhead, Ambleside below Stock, Westmorland, with his wife. Living with them was his brother Richard, an unmarried mariner aged 24 and born in Spalding.

On 4 July 1854 William Royce, a sailor aged 23, married Mary Ann Beeson, aged 22; the groom's father was Joseph, a fisherman.

John Royce was buried on 15 May 1856. His wife Ann was buried before him on 14 October 1835.

On 11 June 1856 Thomas Royce, a mariner aged 25, married Harriet Williamson, aged 24; the groom's father was William, a fisherman.

On 23 August 1857 Joseph Royce, fisherman and a 54-year-old widower, married Hannah King, a widow aged 46; the groom's father was Thomas, a fisherman, and the bride's father was William Hinson, a boatman.

In the 1861 census for vessels, taken at midnight on 7 April, Joseph Royce was Master of the *Mary Ann*, a sloop of 34 tons that was at Broadfleet Sands, Humber; Thomas Royce was Master of the *Mary Ann*, a sloop of 32 tons that was moored at Fosdyke Bridge.

On 10 June 1863 Joseph Royce, a sailor aged 23, married Rebecca Harrison, aged 21; the groom's father was William, a fisherman. They had children Emma (b. 20 February 1864), Joseph (b. 1869), Jane (b. 11 June 1874), Margaret (b. 1 January 1877) and Charlotte (b. 1879). Three of the girls, Emma, Jane and Margaret, were born at Fosdyke and baptised on the same day at All Saints church. Joseph's occupation was given as pilot, and the pilot boat would have been stationed at Fosdyke. In the 1881 census Rebecca Royce, head of the household and a widow, was living at No. 14 Albert Street, Spalding, with Joseph, aged 12, Jane, aged 7, Margaret, aged 4 and Charlotte, aged 2.

The ship *Elizabeth* was a ketch rig of 60 tons. It had the registration number 44770 and its port of registration was Lowestoft. It was built at Wakefield in 1864 and had the international code TWLN. The managing owner was Joseph Royce of No. 42 Commercial Road, Spalding.

On 5 October 1864 Edward Royce, a sailor aged 27, married Elizabeth Smith, aged 26; the groom's father was William, a fisherman.

In 1868 Thomas Royce and Thomas Royce junior received the sum of £16 from the Spalding Shipwreck Society after the vessel *Billow* was destroyed by fire.

On 1 September 1869 Joseph Royce, a sailor aged 20, married Martha Collins, also aged 20.

In the 1871 census William Royce was Master of the sloop *Friends*, which was registered in Boston and was also at Boston at the time of the census.

At the time of the 1881 census Edward Royce, a mariner aged 44, was living with his wife Elizabeth, aged 43, at Albert Street, Spalding.

At the time of the 1881 census William Royce, a mariner aged 30, was living with his wife Alice, aged 30 and born in Aslackby, at No. 42 Commercial Road, Spalding.

At the time of the 1881 census William Royce, an unmarried mariner born in 1856, was living with his mother Elizabeth Royce. Elizabeth, the widow of William, was the head of the household and made her living as a laundress. Also living with her at Holbeach Road, Spalding, were her grandson Thomas, a mariner aged 17, and Jane R., aged 50 and unmarried.

Also listed on the 1881 census is mariner Richard Royce, aged 55 and born in Spalding. He and his wife Margaret, aged 61 and born in Ambleside, Westmorland, were living at No. 44 Strand Road, Bootle cum Linacre, Lancashire.

On the 1891 census John Royce was listed as the mate to Captain Robert Gosterlow on the screw steamer *Nantes*, of 179 tons burden and registered at London.

The Culpin Family

In 'Tales of the Sea', Mrs Turner tells us 'there were many notorious mariners of the Culpin family and Richard Culpin followed Richard Culpin, one generation after another'. I have found a Richard Culpin (1724–92) who married Mary Packstone on 5 May 1748, but I don't have any evidence that he was a mariner. They had children John and Elizabeth, baptised in February 1752; Ann, baptised 1 October 1755 at the age of 2 years and 6 months; Mary, also baptised 1 October 1755, aged 'a quarter' (probably three months); and Richard, baptised 22 February 1764.

Following her husband's death in 1792, Richard's widow Mary married George Eldred, a widower, on 3 December 1794.

Richard and Mary's youngest son, Richard, died at the young age of 23 in 1787. I have not found any other information about him, although I have identified the marriage of a Richard Culpin to Bridget Bains on 8 December 1785 that may be him. Richard and Bridget had a son named Richard, baptised on 3 March 1787. This Richard was recorded as a mariner at the time of his marriage to Maria Gosterlow on 24 September 1810. Her father William was Master and owner of the sloop *Joseph and Ann* in 1831. In November 1831 Richard Culpin was Master and owner of the sloop *Mary Ann*.

As Mrs Turner's story suggests, Richard and Maria had a son, also Richard. At the time of the 1841 census he was living with his parents in Double Street, Spalding. He was aged 25 and a master mariner.

Richard and Maria's second son, William, was a shoemaker and was aged 20 at the the 1841 census. They also had a daughter, Maria, aged 15 in 1841, and a third son, Samuel, also aged 15, who was listed as cabin boy.

On 28 May 1858 Samuel, a mariner, married Ann Dickinson. In 1861 Samuel was master of the sloop *Hope*. Samuel and Ann had children John S. (b. 1860), Maria G. (b. 1862), Richard (b. 1863) and Fredrick (b. 1866). In 1881 Samuel was aged 53 and described as a publican at No. 37 New Road, the Punchbowl. Samuel died on 4 June 1921, aged 94. This last Richard was a stonemason's apprentice in the 1881 census.

On 14 July 1841 Richard and Maria's eldest son Richard married Mary Ann White, the daughter of William White, mariner. White was recorded as the Master and owner of the *Wellington* in March 1833 and Master and owner of the *Ruben* in December 1833. In May 1848 Joseph Gosterlow, mariner, married Eliza, another of William White's daughters, and William's occupation was by now recorded as Harbour Master. This was probably the

Joseph Gosterlow who was Master and owner of a ship called the *Mary Jane*, which went down off the Humber with all hands in 1895 while bringing a cargo of coals from Newcastle to the Spalding gasworks.

Richard and Mary Ann had children Richard (b. 1844), Biddy (b. 1852) and Eliza (b. 1859). At the time of the 1881 census Richard, aged 63, and Mary Ann, aged 61, were living in Commercial Road, Spalding. Their son Richard, a market gardener, and his wife, also Mary Ann, and children Florence, Mary, Ethel and Annie were living at No. 53 London Road, Spalding.

Mrs Turner tells us that one of these Richards was an exceptional character who played all sorts of tricks on various inhabitants when in port. Among his chief victims were the Rev. William Moore DD and his wife, and he had to be severely punished for offending that lady. He also attended a sale at Hull and bid 7s 6d for a carriage. The auctioneer for a joke knocked it down to him, little thinking that a sailor would take it. He then proceeded to sell it again expecting to make £30 to £40 on it; but no, Culpin insisted it was his; it had been lawfully knocked down to him and he meant to have it. It was wheeled on board his vessel and brought home to Spalding. On arrival he borrowed a horse and took all the old ladies of Pigeon End for a ride round the fashionable parts of the town, much to the annoyance of the Johnsons, Moores and other wealthy and influential residents of the town, but to the delight of the occupants, who had never before driven in a carriage.

Richard Culpin, master mariner (husband of Maria Gosterlow), is buried in the cemetery in Pinchbeck Road, Spalding, in a plot in area H. He died on 25 June 1858. On his gravestone is carved the following epitaph:

> My sails are split
> My main mast gone
> My soul has fled the deck
> And here beneath this cold damp stone
> My body lies a wreck.
> But still the promise stands secure
> It shall repeated be
> To sail the seas of endless bliss
> To all eternity.

The Chester Family

A John Chester married to Ann is the first of this family of mariners that I have found. They had a son, also John, born 1826, and a daughter Mary Ann.

A Captain Chester arrived from Stockton on the sloop *May* on 9 April 1843. On 19 April 1843 he sailed from Spalding on the sloop *Lark*, bound for Goole. On 9 May 1853 he arrived from Stockton on the *John and Anne*. In 1856 he was living in Albert Place, Spalding.

His daughter Mary Ann married John Willcox, the son of another Spalding master mariner who owned the sloop *Ebenezer*. The groom's occupation was given as cordwainer (a shoemaker or cobbler).

John Chester (b. 1826) married Sarah Beal on 15 July 1856; her abode was given as Albert Street and his as Commercial Road. He was now a mariner like his father. Her father was a labourer. One witness to the wedding was his sister Mary Ann Willcox. They had a daughter Sarah Jane (b. 1859) and a son John William (b. 1862).

In the 1871 census John Chester is listed as master of the *Beta*, a schooner of 89 tons and registered at Boston, which was at Plymouth when the census was taken.

In the 1872 *White's Directory* of Spalding John Chester is listed as living in Albert Street.

In the 1881 census he is again recorded as Master of the *Beta* and is to be found in Durham. His wife Sarah is living at No. 23c Albert Street with her daughter Sarah Jane, who is unmarried and has a son C.A., aged 8. Their son John William, now aged 19, is living in Broadway, Middlesex, London, and is employed as a shop assistant.

In 1891, the census lists John as a visitor in the household of his niece Sarah Willcox, aged 37, at Park Cottage, Willow Row Walk, Spalding.

In 1901 John Chester, a retired master mariner, is listed on the census at Alexandra House, Castle Terrace, Muswell Hill, Middlesex, London. This is the household of John William Chester and his wife Lillie E. and children Lilian V., aged 8, and Mabel F., who is less than 4 months old.

Finally, in 1911 we find John Chester, a widower aged 84, once again at Park Cottage, Willow Walk, with his niece Sarah Jane Willcox, aged 57, and her sister Annie Willcox, aged 65.

The Hayes Family

The Hayes family can be traced back to at least the 1800s among the Spalding mariners.

I found a record of a Robert Hayes marrying a Margaret Smith on 26 July 1786. They had a son Thomas on 20 November 1789 and another son Robert in October 1791. Margaret died and was buried on 18 October 1791 and Robert died in infancy and was buried on 13 November 1791. Robert married again, to Mary Nunnery, on 16 May 1793. They had a son William (b. 6 June 1794) and a son Robert who was baptised along with William on 21 May 1797. Sadly their father had died before their baptisms; he was buried, aged 34, on 10 January 1797.

An earlier John Hayes died in 1797 aged 63, but I can find no record of him being a mariner.

In 1825 a John Hayes married Ann Abbott. The next time I find this John Hayes is in the *Boston Ships Register* on 31 August 1833 as Master of the sloop *Wellington*. In the *Boston Ships Register* on 17 February 1834 John Hayes is listed as Master of the sloop *Bee*.

In 1840 John Hayes, a widower, married Eliza Webster. Unfortunately his father's Christian name is illegible; however, both the groom and his father are mariners.

On the 1841 census John and Ann are recorded as having a son, John, who is 5 years old. They are the home of William Barnard in London Road, Boston.

In the 1842 *White's Directory* of Spalding a John Hayes, mariner, was living in Holbeach Road, Spalding.

In 1844 the Spalding Shipwreck Society was formed; John Hayes senior was a founder member.

When the 1851 census was taken, John Hayes, master mariner, and his wife Ann were at London Road, Boston.

In 1860 their son John Hayes junior married Elizabeth Healey. His occupation and his father's are both given as 'sailor'.

In the 1861 census for vessels at sea, the record for the schooner *Melita* gives John Hayes senior, aged 50, as Master, and Robert Hayes, aged 22, as mate. Also in 1861, the census record for the sloop *Anne* gives John Hayes junior, aged 24, as Master, and William Hayes, aged 17, as boy.

In 1872 John junior received the sum of £8 from the Spalding Shipwreck Society for partial loss of clothing due to the sinking of the vessel *Mary Catherine*.

On the 1881 census John's wife Elizabeth is recorded as living at No. 33 Albert Street, Spalding, with daughters Edith, aged 14, Agnes, aged 13, and a son William, aged 9. The household also contains an unmarried brother Robert Hayes, aged 42, a sailor.

In September 1881 Robert Hayes married Elizabeth Ouzerman Walker, widow, in Edmonton, London. In 1886 they had a daughter Ellen. Elizabeth died in March 1887 at the age of 49.

At the time of the 1891 census John junior was aged 64 and was living with his wife Elizabeth aged 67, at No. 33 Albert Street, Spalding. His occupation is listed as coal merchant. His brother Robert was living at No. 13 Commercial Road, Spalding and is described as a retired mariner. In the household are his daughter Ellen, aged 15, stepdaughter Elizabeth Walker, aged 31, and a housekeeper.

John junior died in 1912.

In April 1906 Robert Hayes was a witness at the wedding of my grandparents Herbert Seaton and Edith Ada Vine.

Two other Hayes brothers, Robert Arthur and John William, owned the steamer *Speedwell*, which traded along the east coast until it was bought by the Admiralty during the First World War and used as a part of Hull's boom defences.

The Knott Family

This family has been difficult to research due to the Christian names being used over and over again. Tragically many of the family's mariners were lost at sea. When looking for them in the census records they are often missing as they were away at sea and the wife is given as the head of the family.

Thomas Knott, mariner, married Mary Hudson at Gainsborough on 16 May 1817. They had a daughter Mary (b. 1818) and four sons: John (b. 1822), Henry (b. 1826), Thomas (b. 1831) and William (b. 1835).

Thomas was lost at sea off Scarborough on 20 December 1837 at the age of 48.

In the 1841 census a Henry Knott, aged 15 – presumably the son of Thomas and Mary – was living with Eleanor Knott aged 50 in Albion Street, Spalding. Eleanor was the wife of Charles Knott, whom she had married on 14 April 1805. She was a member of the Gosterlow family, one of Spalding's major maritime families, and was probably Henry's aunt. Henry was lost at sea off Dimlington on 17 January 1842, at the age of 17.

Thomas and Mary's oldest son John Knott, mariner, married Eliza Wilson on 20 June 1844 at the church of St Mary and St Nicholas, Spalding. The groom's father's occupation was given as mariner.

In the 1851 census Elizabeth was living at Willow Row, Spalding with their five children Henry, aged 5, John, aged 4, Thomas, aged 2, Milicent, aged 1, and William, aged 1 month.

Spalding Ships News in the *Spalding Free Press* on 5 May 1851 states that the *Mary and S. Marsden* and Captain Knott sailed for Newcastle.

The third son of Thomas and Mary, Thomas Knott, was lost at sea in the Bristol Channel on 24 November 1852 at the age of 22.

In Spalding Ships News on 17 January 1853 the *Mary and S. Marsden* and Captain Knott arrived from Newcastle with coals.

In the 1861 census listing of vessels at sea, the *Mary and S. Marsden*, a sloop of 39 tons, is recorded as resting in Hawk Roads. John Knott, aged 38, is listed as Master and Henry Knott, aged 16, as boy.

In the 1861 census John's wife Eliza is recorded as living at Willow Row, Spalding, with their children Thomas, aged 12, Millicent, aged 11, William, aged 10, Wilson, aged 7, Priscilla, aged 5, and Mary A., aged 8 months.

John Knott drowned in the River Thames on 20 May 1869, aged 46.

In the 1871 census of vessels at sea, *Rapid*, a schooner of 57 tons, registered at Boston, is anchored at Grays Reach, River Thames. Henry Knott, aged 25, is listed as Master and Wilson Knott, aged 17, as able seaman.

Also listed on the 1871 census is Richard Knott, aged 30, mate on the sloop *Friends*, which is anchored at Skirbeck Quarter, Boston. I am not sure if this Richard is related to Thomas and Mary.

The 1871 census records Mary Knott, aged 78, as living in Holbeach Road, Spalding. The household also includes her son William, aged 36, mariner, and her granddaughter Priscilla, aged 15.

Mary Knott, Thomas's widow, died in Spalding, aged 83, on 2 July 1876.

The youngest son of Thomas and Mary, William, was also in the mercantile marine. He erected a tombstone to his father and brothers in Spalding cemetery; he was also lost at sea. The *Spalding Free Press* of 20 May 1884 reported:

The *Buckinghamshire* of London that left Shields for Rangoon (Yangon) with coals on October 2nd 1883 was spoken to in Latitude. 21 N Longitude. 40 W on January 7th. (The Chief mate William Knott of Spalding) was on last Wednesday posted at Lloyds as missing. We have reason to fear that the ship has been lost with all hands.

William Knott's Second Mate's Certificate.

The Draper Family

The Draper family were another Spalding family of shipowners and master mariners in the first half of the 1800s.

Thomas Draper was Master and owner of the sloop *Industry* when it was registered in the *Boston Ships Register* in 1824 and the sloop *Glen* in 1826.

The *Glen* and Captain Draper are listed in 'Spalding Shipping News' as arriving from London with goods on 22 December 1830 and again on 13 April 1831. The *Glen* sailed with oats and flour on 20 April 1831 and on several further occasions in 1831 to London with corn, oats and flour, also returning with goods. This Thomas was married to Ann (maiden name not found); they had a son, also Thomas (b. 1821), daughters Mary Jane (b. 1824) and Ann (b. 1826), and another son Richard (b. 1829).

Thomas is in the 1842 directory listed as master mariner, and in 1856 he was living in Albion Street at the Ship Albion. He is known to have been the landlord there from as early as 1850, when the Shipwreck Society established its headquarters there and he was their president. Thomas died in 1864, aged 74.

Mary Jane married Edward Todd Richardson, shipbuilder of King's Lynn, Norfolk, on 10 February 1843. His father was Andrew Young Richardson, shipbuilder.

The younger Thomas Draper married Rebecca King on 29 January 1846. His father is given as Thomas Draper senior, master mariner. Rebecca's father is given as Thomas King, publican. He was landlord of the Ship Active, also in Albion Street.

Thomas and Rebecca had the following children: Richard (b. 1846), Rebecca Ann (b. 1849 – she married my great-grandfather John Henry Vine on 12 May 1870), George Thomas (b. 1851), Eliza Jane (b. 1852), William Henry (b. 1853), Thomas (b. 1855), Ellen King (b. 1856), Sarah Hannah (b. 1858 – she married Captain John Richard Grassam), Lucy Charlotte (b. 1860), Ada Mary (b. 1861) and Clara Alice (b. 1863).

Thomas was Master of the sloop *Urania* in 1849. In the *Boston Ships Register* the vessel's owner is recorded as Thomas Draper. When Richard and Rebecca Ann were baptised in 1846 and 1849, Thomas is listed as mariner, but by 1851, when George Thomas was baptised, he is a publican, having taken over the Ship Albion from his father.

Thomas died aged 65 and was buried on 8 May 1886.

The Atkin Family

In Mrs Turner's 'Tales of the Sea' we are told that the Atkin family was another fine old family that for many generations followed the sea.

I found a John Atkin who was described as a labourer in 1842 and 1844, a higgler in 1848 and a housekeeper in 1853, on the marriages of four sons who were all mariners at the time of their weddings: William, Robert, Joseph and James.

The first to marry was William, whose wedding to Elizabeth Sarah East took place on 28 August 1842. I cannot find any children from this marriage and can only find one record of a William Atkin in the shipping records, a seaman on the sloop *Samuel* in 1871.

Robert married Sarah Taylor on 4 August 1844. They had children Robert, baptised 25 December 1846, and James, baptised on 21 January 1849. In 1871 Robert was the mate of the schooner *Olive*, crossing Kent. In 1881 he is the first officer of the screw steamer *Artos* at Dunkerque, France.

Joseph married Mary Towers on 7 August 1848. They had children Joseph, baptised 25 August 1848 (only eighteen days after their wedding), Joseph William, baptised 6 June 1860, and John Richard, baptised 29 September 1865. Joseph was recorded as captain of the sloop *Elizabeth* in Edward Fisher's ledger in 1860 and as master of the *Elizabeth* on the 1861 census, when he was living at No. 13 Marsh Road, Spalding. In following directories and censuses he is still a master mariner living at Marsh Road and from 1881 until 1905 he is Harbour Master and still living at Marsh Road. He died on 12 February 1908 and is buried in Spalding cemetery.

James married Elizabeth Osborn on 28 September 1853. Elizabeth died on 29 March 1860 aged 28 and is buried in Spalding cemetery, along with one child who died in infancy. In 1861 James was listed as a master mariner, aged 35 and a widower, living with Rebecca Osborn aged 25, housekeeper, and his children James Charles aged 3, who was baptised on 24 February 1858, and Elizabeth aged 1. His eldest son William George aged 5, who was baptised on 3 October 1858, is living next door with his grandparents Joseph and Elizabeth Osborn.

James Atkin's Master's Certificate.

Spalding Shipwreck Society mariner members around 1910. Back row, second from right: Captain J. Turner. Front row, left to right: -?-, Captain E. Royce, Captain S. Culpin, Captain G. Levesley, Captain Chester, Captain Hayes, -?-.

James married Rebecca at King's Lynn in 1861, and they went on to have several children: Martha Jane (b. 13 January 1864), Frances Sarah (b. 17 December 1865), Fredrick Edwin (b. 30 July 1874) and Ernest Arthur (b. 30 June 1879).

James is recorded as captain of the sloop *Samuel* from 1861 to 1864 in the ledger of the blacksmith Edward Fisher, and on the 1871 census he is also listed as Master of the *Samuel*, which is moored in the Goole Canal. Rebecca is living with children James Charles aged 13, Elizabeth aged 11 and Francis J. aged 5.

His home address in the *Kelly's Directory* of 1885 is Albion Street. In 1892 he is listed in *White's Directory* as a barge owner at No. 29 Albert Street.

James Atkin, master mariner, died on 22 November 1893, aged 70, and is buried in Spalding cemetery.

James Charles, son of James and Elizabeth, married Harriet Tagg in March 1882. He was master of the sloop *John*, which on the 1881 census was recorded at Hull Harbour and on the 1891 census at Methley. In *White's Directory* of 1892 he is listed as living at No. 19a Willow Walk and then in

1905 at Fern Cottage, Albert Street. Fern Cottage was named after the vessel *Fern*, which was one of the last sailing vessels trading out of the port of Spalding. In the *Spalding Guardian* on Friday 6 February 1981, Mr Frank Darnes recalled his father Mr Harold Darnes talking of a trip he made with Captain Atkin in 1910 when he was 10 years old. This return trip to Keadby Bridge on the River Trent took two or three days on the *Fern*. Mr Darnes's family lived next door to Fern Cottage in Albert Street.

John Grundy junior 1719–83

Although he was not a mariner, John Grundy junior was a shipowner and a famous resident of Spalding; as such I felt that he should be included in this chapter.

John Grundy junior, the engineer, was the son of John Grundy senior, the agent of the honourable adventurers of Deeping Great Fen. Grundy junior succeeded his father in this post. He lived in Spalding in a house that he built on the bank of the River Welland with a landing stage, timber yard, oil mill and warehouses. He owned the sloop *Good Intent*, which voyaged to the Baltic for timber, and a lighter, *Polly and Lydia*, named after his two surviving children, which carried cargoes of corn, rapeseed and coal to and from larger vessels anchored at Fosdyke near the Welland outfall into the Wash.

At the age of 20, his earliest work was a sluice near the outfall of the Blue Goat Drain into the River Glen. Later he built a staunch (a dam with an opening through which craft could pass) on the River Welland as part of the Stamford Navigation.

As a surveyor and drainage engineer he made a feasibility survey for the navigation from Tetney Haven – on the coast of north Lincolnshire, a few miles south of Grimsby and Cleethorpes– to Louth, using part of the River Ludd. This navigation was started in 1765 and completed through to Louth in 1770. It was one of the earliest canal schemes in England.

He also submitted a plan to create a grand sluice by placing doors below the town bridge as part of the improvement scheme for the River Witham at Boston. A revised plan for this sluice, which was built by Langley Edwards, was approved by Grundy and his friend John Smeaton (famous for the building of the Eddystone Lighthouse). The sluice was finally opened in 1766 and was then the largest of its kind in Britain.

He continued worked on drainage and canal construction in South Yorkshire throughout his career, including work on the Driffield Navigation

The Boston Grand Sluice from upstream, with sloops, keels and a steam tug. This image possibly dates from the early 1800s.

Mr Grundy's warehouse before it was demolished for road improvements in January 1973.

from Frodingham Beck to Driffield, completed in 1770, and planning the wet dock at Hull that was to become the first Hull Dock.

He was said to have been perhaps the first civil engineer in this country to have been trained for the profession. He was a member of Spalding Gentlemen's Society and a founder member of the Society of Civil Engineers. After his death he was buried in Spalding parish church in the family vault. There is a commemorative plaque to John Grundy junior on the wall inside the north door of the church, on the left-hand side.

6

Boston Ships Registers 1824–92: Spalding and District Masters and Owners

The measurement rule and registration for tonnage from 1720 was the length of the keel minus the greatest breadth (beam) and that product multiplied by three-fifths then multiplied by half the breadth; then the last product divided by 94. The quotient gave the tonnage required for a merchant ship. In 1849 a commission was set up, with Admiral George Moorsom as secretary, to look into the rule and it was changed to include the depth from gunwale to keel. The Moorsom rule, simplified, was the length overall multiplied by the greatest breadth multiplied by the maximum depth plus one-third divided by 70 to give the tonnage:

SUCCESS
Registered 15 April 1824; Zachariah Potts, Master.

Sloop, carvel built, lifting bowsprit. Length overall, 60' 2", beam 17'
= 73 45/94 tons.

Owner Thomas Potts of Boston; registration No. 40540.

This sloop visited Spalding from Hull on 26 October 1831, Captain Hossell, with goods, deals and linseed cakes.

BETSY
Registered 9 June 1824; John Barker, Master.

Sloop, clincher built, topping up bowsprit.[1] Length overall 52', beam 15'2"
= 50 42/94 tons.

Owner Thomas Rosbe, Spalding; registration No. 40681.

---

1 A lifting or topping-up bowsprit was necessary to reduce the length needed for mooring up to unload cargo when in port.

Sloop *Success* outward bound from the River Welland, from a painting by F.W. Birch. (Reproduced by kind permission of Mr Stewart Ingle)

BLESSING

Registered 5 November 1825; John Royce, Master.

Sloop, clincher built, topping up bowsprit. Length overall 56' 10", beam 14'
= 48 38/94 tons.

Owner John Markille of Spalding; registration No. 40682.

November 1826, John Royce, Master & owner.

INDUSTRY

Registered November 1824; Thomas Draper, Master.

Sloop, clincher built, topping up bowsprit. Length overall 55'8, beam 14'
= 47 56/94 tons.

Owner Thomas Draper of Spalding.

December 1826, Joseph Collins, Master.

EBENEZER

Registered April 1825; John Willcox, Master.

Sloop, clincher built, topping up bowsprit. Length overall 56' 6", beam 14'3"
= 50 38/94 tons.

Owner John Willcox of Spalding.

TWO BROTHERS

Registered 8 November 1825; Edward Jackson, Master.

Sloop, clincher built, topping up bowsprit. Length overall 55'52, beam 14'
= 47 91/94 tons.

Owner Thomas Smith of Spalding.

GLEN

Registered 2 February 1826; Thomas Draper, Master.

Sloop, carvel & clincher built, topping up bowsprit. Length overall 59'4",
beam 16'11" = 72 70/94 tons.

Owner Thomas Draper of Spalding.

ANN & ELIZABETH

Registered March 1826; William Jarvis, Master.

Sloop, clincher built, topping up bowsprit, length overall 50'6", beam 14'2"
= 43 80/94 tons.

Owner William Gosterlow of Spalding.

UNION

Registered March 1826; William Butler, Master.

Sloop, clincher built, topping up bowsprit. Length overall 47'6", beam 14'1"
= 40 62/94 tons.

Owner John Moats of Spalding.

NANCY

Registered July 1826; John Turpin, Master.

Sloop, clincher built, topping up bowsprit. Length overall 58', beam 14'1"
= 50 40/94 tons.

Owner John Turpin of Spalding.

THOMAS & ELIZABETH

Registered November 1826; Charles Breasley, Master.

Sloop, clincher built, topping up bowsprit. Length overall 57'3", beam 14'1"
= 42 89/94 tons.

Owner Thomas Rosbe of Spalding.

CHARLOTTE & ELIZABETH

Registered November 1826; Richard Culpin, Master.

Sloop, clincher built, topping up bowsprit. Length overall 51'10", beam
13'1" = 42 85/94 tons.

Owner, Richard Culpin of Spalding.

WELLAND

Registered 6 December 1827; Thomas Knott, Master.

Sloop, clincher built, topping up bowsprit. Length overall 56'6", beam 14'2"
= 50 tons.

Owner Thomas Knott of Spalding.

WILLIAM

Registered November 1827; William Johnson, Master.

Sloop, clincher built, topping up bowsprit. Length overall 50'6", beam 13'2½" = 38 60/94 tons.

Owner William Johnson of Spalding.

MAYFLOWER

Registered November 1827, William Gregory, Master.

Sloop, clincher built, topping up bowsprit. Length overall 48'1", beam 15'3" = 47 tons.

Owner William Gregory of Spalding.

TWO BROTHERS

Registered November 1827; Edward Jackson, Master.

Sloop, clincher built, topping up bowsprit. Length overall 55'5", beam 14' = 47 91/94 tons.

Owners Thomas Smith & Robert Brown of Spalding.

JANE

Registered April 1827; William Gosterlow, Master.

Sloop, clincher built, topping up bowsprit. Length overall 54'10", beam 15'8" = 58 tons.

Owner William Gosterlow of Spalding.

ELIZABETH

Registered June 1827; Edward Seymour, Master.

Sloop, clincher built, topping up bowsprit. Length overall 50'10", beam 15'3" = 50 88/94 tons.

Owner Matthew Thorpe of Spalding.

ALBION

Registered December 1827; built at Boston by Richardson's, December 1827; Thomas Wilkinson jnr, Master.

Sloop, clincher built, topping up bowsprit. Length overall 53'2", beam 14'4" = 46 60/94 tons.

Owner James Markille of Spalding.

1833, John Pakey, Master.

ANCHOLME

Registered 8 April 1828.

Sloop, clincher built. Length overall 57'2", beam 15'6" = 50 7/94 tons.

4 December 1833, William Butler, Master.

PRINCE REGENT

Registered June 1828; Francis Parnell, Master.

Sloop, carvel built, fixed bowsprit. Length overall 54'4", beam 16'11" = 65 78/94 tons.

Owner Charles Bonner of Spalding.

SPEEDWELL
Registered February 1829; William Wilson Hayes, Master.

Sloop, clincher built, topping up bowsprit. Length overall 45'6", beam 14'10" = 42 33/94 tons.

Owner William Wilson Hayes of Spalding.

UNITY
Registered April 1829; John Rear, Master.

Sloop, clincher built, topping up bowsprit. Length overall 47'2", beam 14'4½" = 47 46/94 tons.

Owner John Rear.

SPALDING
Registered November 1829; William Green, Master.

Sloop, topping up bowsprit. Length overall 49'8", beam, 13'10" = 40 38/94 tons.

Owners Thomas Rear & William Green of Spalding.

COMMERCE
Registered 15 September 1828; built at Newcastle, Henry Butler, Master.[1]

Sloop, clincher built, topping up bowsprit. Length overall 51', beam, 13'9" = 45 79/94 tons.

Owner Thomas Wilkinson.

BEE
Registered 24 December 1828; built at Boston by Andrew Richardson; Peter Royce, Master.

Sloop, clincher built, topping up bowsprit. Length overall 53'2", beam 14'10" = 45 88/94 tons.

Owners Andrew Richardson, Roger Banks, & Peter Royce.

17 February 1834, John Hayes, Master.

SPALDING
Registered 13 November 1829; William Green, Master.

Sloop, clincher build, topping up bowsprit. Length overall 49'8", beam 13'10" = 40 38/94 tons.

Owners Thomas Rear & John Green of Spalding.

WELLAND
Registered 12 July 1830; built at Louth, James Rogerson, Master.

Sloop, clincher built. Length overall 56'6", beam 6'1" = 50 15/94 tons.

Owner John Mears of Gedney.

May 1831, James Rogerson, owner.

---

1 Father-in-law to Matthew Southwell Vine.

ENDEAVOURS INCREASE

Registered September 1830.

Built at Spalding, Richard Wilkinson, Master.

Sloop, clincher built, topping up bowsprit. Length overall 47'6", beam 14'
    = 39 67/94 tons.

Owners Thomas Smith & Robert Proctor of Spalding.

1832, William Allen, Master & owner.

JOSEPH & ANN

Registered 9 February 1831; William Gosterlow, Master.

Sloop, clincher built, topping up bowsprit. Length overall 56'7", beam 14'2"
    = 50 66/94 tons.

Owner William Gosterlow of Spalding.

MARY ANN

Registered 15 November 1831; Richard Culpin, Master.

Sloop, clincher built, topping up bowsprit. Length overall 56'6", beam 14'1"
    = 49 9/94 tons.

Owner Richard Culpin of Spalding.

UNITY

Registered 14 June 1832; John Royce, Master.

Sloop, carvel built, topping up bowsprit. Length overall 47'2", beam 15'4½"
    = 47 46/94 tons.

Owners John Moats & William Gosterlow.

1834, George Morris, Master.

1835, Charles Buyton, Master.

FRIENDSHIP

Registered 16 January 1833; John Royce, Master.

Sloop, carvel built, topping up bowsprit, length overall 56', beam 13'10"
    = 50 50/94 tons.

Owners, John Royce & John Seymour of Spalding.

ELIZABETH

Registered 15 March 1833; built at Spalding, Edward Seymour, Master.

Sloop, clincher built, topping up bowsprit, length overall 50'2", beam 15'3"
    = 50 88/94 tons.

Owner, Edward Seymour.

Certificate cancelled 17 April 1833.

Re-registered, April 1833.

John Jackson, master. Owners, Clark Seymour & Joseph Tupman of
    Surfleet.

WELLINGTON

Registered 16 March 1833; John White, Master.

Sloop, clincher built, topping up bowsprit, length overall 58'1", beam 16'5" = 66 53/94 tons.

Owner, William White of Spalding.

31 August 1833, John Hayes, Master.

3 October 1835, John White, Master.

GOOD INTENT

Registered 5 June 1833; built at Spalding, William Hope, Master.

Sloop, carvel built, topping up bowsprit, length overall 44'7", beam 15'3" = 43 67/94 tons.

Owner, Henry Smith of Stamford.

NEW GOOD INTENT

Registered 14 June 1833; built at Burton on Stather by John Wray; William Burton, Master.

Sloop, carvel built, topping up bowsprit, length overall 57'1", beam, 17'8" = 75 34/94 tons.

Owners, William Burton of Spalding, & William Beckford & John Hobson.

FREEDOM

Registered 17 December 1833; built at Knottingley, Yorkshire; John Royce, Master.

Sloop, carvel & clincher built, topping up bowsprit, length overall 57'3", beam 14'3" = 51 20/94 tons.

Owners, John Royce of Spalding & Thomas Dickinson of Surfleet.

RUBEN

Registered 19 December 1833; built at Wakefield, Yorkshire, 23 August 1832; William White, Master.

Sloop, carvel & clincher built, topping up bowsprit, length overall 59', beam 16'9¼" =72 23/94 tons.

Owner William White of Spalding.

METCALF

Registered 1834. Built at Wimlington, Yorkshire, William Jarvis, Master.

Sloop, carvel & clincher built, topping up bowsprit, length overall 56'1", beam 15'6" = 61 15/94 tons.

Owner, Richard Carter of Gosberton.

MARY & ANN

Registered 14 April 1834; built at Louth; John Bartrup, Master.

Sloop, clincher built, topping up bowsprit, length overall 56'9", beam 14'½" = 49 25/94 tons.

Owner John Bartrup of Spalding.

24 October 1834, Elizabeth Bartrup, widow of John Bartrup, transferred the
bill of sale to William Parnham of Moulton Seas End.

CETO

Registered 15 December 1834; built at Boston; John Rear, Master.

Sloop, clincher built, topping up bowsprit. Length overall 47'7", beam 14'1"
= 41 43/94 tons.

Owner John Rear of Spalding.

BROTHERS & SISTERS

Registered 29 December 1834; built at Boston; James Audlin, Master.

Sloop, carvel built, topping up bowsprit, length overall 51'3", beam, 12'3"
= 35 3/94 tons.

Owners James Audlin & William Audlin of Spalding.

13 May 1836, John Atkin, Master.

THOMAS & JANE

Registered 29 December 1834; built at Lincoln 1820; John Seymour, Master.

Sloop, clincher built, length overall 56'8", beam, 14'½" = 49 47/94 tons.

Owner John Seymour of Spalding.

BLESSING

Registered 27 May 1836; William Southwell, Master.[1]

Sloop, clincher built, length overall 53'8", beam 12'6½" = 36 tons.

Owner William Southwell.

8 October 1849, William Butler, Master.

20 September 1850, Jno Turner, Master.

JOHN & JANE

Registered 1836; built at Boston; John Booth, Master.

Sloop, clincher built, length overall 49', beam 11'9" = 19 tons.

Owner John Booth of Spalding.

WSR

Registered January 1846; Thomas Duckering, Master.

Sloop, lifting bowsprit, length overall 51', beam 14' = 57 7/10 tons.

Owner Thomas Duckering of Spalding.

3 April 1849, George Crooks, owner, William Crooks, Master.

URANIA

Registered January 1849; built at Boston, Thomas Draper jnr, Master.

Sloop, length overall 56'6", beam 14', depth 6' = 53 6/10 tons.

Owner Thomas Draper of Spalding.

---

1 Matthew Southwell Vine's mother's maiden name was Elizabeth Southwell.

BREEZE

Registered January 1849; built at Brigg by Edward and Samuel Womack, 4 December 1848; George Levesley, Master.

Sloop, carvel & clincher, topping up bowsprit, length overall 57'2/10, beam 13' 6/10, depth, 7' = 53 77/350 tons.

Part-owner George Levesley of Spalding, 64 shares.

10 May 1854, re-registered; length overall 59' 7/10, beam 15' 6/10, depth 7'9/10 = 68 tons.

22 October 1870, vessel altered from sloop to ketch; registration No. 621.

METCALF

Registered 24 May 1849; John Collins, Master.

Sloop, carvel & clincher built, topping up bowsprit, length overall 53'7/10, beam 14'2/10, depth 5'8/10 = 64 tons.

Owner George Crooks of Spalding.

25 July 1853, Edward Turner, Master.

SAMUEL BARNARD

Registered 22 September 1849; built at Kingston upon Hull, 1836; George Johnson of Spalding, Master & owner.

Schooner, carvel built, two masts, length overall 58'2/10, beam 15'6/10, depth 8' = 71 tons.

5 April 1855, George Gulliford, Master & owner. Re-registered at Stockton, No. 6205.

16 March 1858, James Poppleton, owner.

13 September 1860, William James Sharman, owner.

27 September 1860, Robert Dawbarn, owner.

23 January 1861, Matthew S. Vine, owner, and Joseph Vine, Master.

3 September 1868, John Thresh, owner.

Lost at Sea near the South Pier of the Tyne.

PROVIDENCE

Registered 27 March 1850; built at Mexbrough, Yorkshire, 1848; John Taylor, Master.

Sloop, length overall 52'8/10, beam 12'3/10, depth 4' = 47½ tons.

Owner John Taylor of Spalding with John Smith of Fosdyke.

17 April 1860, William Ellis of Spalding, owner.

13 November 1861, lost with all hands.

URANIA

Registered 13 May 1853; Joseph Gosterlow, Master.

Sloop, carvel & clincher, topping up bowsprit, length overall 56'6/10, beam 14', depth 6' 6/10 = 52 tons.

Owner Joseph Gosterlow.

JANE

Re-registered 1846; Robert Jackson, Master.

Sloop, clincher built, length overall 53', beam 14'4", depth 5' = 42 tons

Owner John Payne.

16 February 1847, John Weatherall, Master.

22 July 1847, Robert Payne, Master.

19 July 1849, John Weatherall, Master.

12 July 1850, Isaac Gosterlow, Master.

21 October 1850, Henry Colley, Master.

ANCHOLME

Re-registered 5 August 1846; James Clark, Master.

Sloop, length overall 53' 3/10, beam 12' 4/10, depth 4' = 34 39/100 tons.
Owner Mary Ann Hill.

22 January 1847, John Hubbard, Master.

1 January 1852, John Greenhall, Master & owner.

ELLEN

Registered 17 March 1847; William Crooks, Master.

Sloop, carvel and clincher built, topping up bowsprit, length overall 53' 8/10,
beam 12' 6/10, depth 6' = 417/10 tons.

Owner George Crooks; registered No. 4892.

24 February 1849, Joseph Vine, Master.

7 May 1853, Edward Turner, Master.

26 July 1853, George Kidd, Master.

11 September 1857, sold to Joseph Willcock of Wakefield.

TWO SISTERS

Registered 14 November 1846; John Pakey, Master & owner.

Sloop, clincher built, lifting bowsprit, length overall 54' 9/10, beam 12' 5/10,
depth 5' = 38 tons.

JOHN AND ANN

Registered 27 March 1847; John Seymour, Master & owner.

Schooner, clincher and carvel, topping up bowsprit, length overall 57' 7/10,
beam 14' 3/10, Depth, 6' 5/10 = 53 tons.

13 December 1848, Thomas Royce, Master.

24 July 1851, John Seymour, Master.

1 March 1853, John Chester, Master.

27 March 1854, John Seymour transferred the bill of sale, drafted on
4 October 1853, 64 shares unto Matthew S. Vine of Spalding.

MARY ANN

Registered 26 May 1847; Richard Culpin, Master & owner.

Sloop, clincher built, topping up bowsprit, length overall 53' 8/10, beam 12' 7/10, depth 6' 5/10 = 36 tons.

21 March 1849, Richard Culpin, Master & owner.

MARY & S MARSDEN

Registered 31 May 1847; John Knott, Master.

Sloop, clincher built, topping up bowsprit, length overall 55' 8/10, beam 19' 3/10, depth 6' 3/10 = 39 tons.

Owner, George Crooks; Registration No. 3602.

SISTERS

Registered 21 July 1847; Samuel Belcham, Master & owner.

Sloop, clincher built, topping up bowsprit, length overall 54', beam 12' 7/10, depth, 5' 5/10 = 33 tons.

Registration No. 4823;

2 August 1848, William Ellis, Master & owner.

MARY

Registered 21 August 1847; Isaac Greenhall, Master & owner.

Sloop, carvel and clincher built, topping up bowsprit, length overall 53' 7/10, beam 12' 6/10, depth 5' 5/10 = 29 tons.

Registration No. 6323;

AURORA

Registered 19 October, 1847; built at Spalding in 1847; Benjamin Draper, Master.

Sloop, clincher and carvel, length overall 57', beam 14' 5/10, depth 6' 5/10 = 50 tons.

Owners Thomas and Benjamin Draper.

18 April 1848, Joseph Richardson, Master.

6 May 1848, Edward Richardson, Master.

31 May 1852, re-registered; Edward Richardson Master & owner; registration No. 23630.

14 February 1854, Thomas Mariat, Master.

7 January 1878, re-registered; owners Thomas & William Royce. Thomas died 9 November 1878 and ownership passed to William Royce, Harriet Royce, John Turner & Charles Bower.

3 November 1881, the vessel stranded on the Black Midden Rocks at Tynmouth at 5 p.m. The crew were saved but the cargo and documents were all lost.

PROVIDENCE

Built by John Shuttleworth of Boston; George Booth, Master & owner.

Keel, clincher built, no bowsprit, length overall 15' 5/10, beam 11' 5/10, depth 3' – 15 tons.

28 April 1870, broken up.

VIOLET

Registered 3 May 1848; Joseph Dunn, Master & owner.

Sloop, clincher built, topping up bowsprit, length overall 51' 4/10, beam 13' 2/10, depth 5' 5/10 = 31 tons.

Registered No. 4897.

BILLOW

Registered 20 February 1851; Henry Walker, Master & owner.

Schooner, carvel built, standing bowsprit. length overall 66' 3/10, beam 17' 2/10, depth 10' = 85 tons.

Registered No. 2008;.

DAVID AND ANN

Registered 5 July 1851; Thomas Royce, Master.

Sloop, carvel built, topping up bowsprit; length overall 55', beam 13' 7/10; depth, 5' 7/10 = 40 tons.

Owner Susannah Wilkinson.

31 May 1856, sunk in Lynn Well on the 18 May last and totally lost; signed by Susannah Wilkinson (X) her mark and certified by Thomas Royce, late Master.

SEA

Registered 15 January 1852; William Hugh Macoman, Master.

Sloop, clincher and carvel built, topping up bowsprit. length overall 57' 6/10, beam, 12' 9/10, depth 6' 6/10 = 47 tons.

Owner Thomas Draper.

10 September 1853, John Greenhall, Master.

WELLINGTON

Registered 14 February 1852; John Hubbard, Master.

Sloop, clincher built, topping up bowsprit, length overall 54' 4/10, beam 12' 7/10, depth, 5' 7/10 = 39 tons.

Registration No. 4795.

15 September 1853, James Atkin, Master.

POLLY

Registered 6 March 1852; John Payne, Master & owner.

Schooner, carvel built, standing bowsprit, length overall 65', beam 13' 4/10, depth 10' 6/10 = 86 tons.

24 November 1852, vessel lost off Hayle, Cornwall together with the Master who was sole owner and two of her crew. Declaration given by Henry Hoskins, one of the crew saved.

URANIA

Re-registered; Joseph Gosterlow, Master & owner.

Sloop, carvel and clincher, topping up bowsprit, length overall 56' 6/10, beam 14' 3/10, depth 6' 6/10 = 42 tons.

Registration No. 23337.

EAGLE

Registered 14 September 1853; John Taylor, Master & owner.

Sloop, clincher built, topping up bowsprit. length overall 53' 4/10, beam 12' 7/10, depth, 5' 9/10 = 39 tons.

Registration No. 11352.

GLEN

Re-registered 21 September 1853; Henry Wilkinson, Master & owner.

Sloop, carvel and clincher, standing bowsprit, length overall 55', beam 15' 2/10, depth 7' 2/10 = 49 tons.

Registration No. 25392.

SEA

New registration, 5 November 1853; John Greenhall, Master & owner.

Sloop, carvel and cincher, topping up bowsprit. length overall 57' 6/10, beam 12' 9/10, depth 6' 6/10 = 41 tons.

Registration No. 9013.

1860, lost at sea

MARY ANN

Registered 9 January 1854;.

Sloop, clincher built, topping up bowsprit, length overall 53' 8/10, beam 12' 7/10, depth 6' 2/10 = 36 tons.

Registered at London No. 100.

JOHN AND ANN

Registered 27 March 1854; built at Goole; Matthew Southwell Vine, Master & owner.

Schooner, carvel and clincher built, topping up bowsprit, length overall 57' 7/10, beam 14' 3/10, Depth, 6' 5/10 = 53 tons.

Registration No. 11802;.

SARAH

Registered 8 July 1857, built City of Lincoln 1842.

Sloop, length overall 60' 3/10, beam 15' 2/10, depth 6' 5/10 = 40 tons.

James Poppleton, owner; registration No. 4796.

8 February 1862, sold to Thomas Royce.

9 November 1878, Thomas Royce died and ownership passed to Harriet Royce & John Turner. John Turner was owner after Harriet died in 1883 until it was sold to Henry Batteman Massey (engineer) on 27 July 1894. He sold it to Arthur Robinson of Grimsby on 11 October 1894.

JOHN AND JUNE

Built 1796.

Sloop, length overall 51' 6/10, beam 13' 6/10, depth 4' 1/10 = 17 tons.

Joseph Woodward, owner.

9 August 1874, Joseph Woodward died. Vessel sold by his wife Rebecca to Charles Fulcher Lincoln of Wisbech on 11 November 1874, who then sold her to John Kingston of Fosdyke on 2 August 1877.

7 January 1878, certificate cancelled. To be used for Inland navigation only.

RED ROVER

Registered 21 May 1857; built 20 May 1857; George Levesley, Master.

Sloop, carvel built, length overall 48' 7/10, beam 12' 9/10, depth 5' 7/10 = 17 tons.

Owner Henry Bugg; registration No. 10399.

24 December 1860, cancelled at the Port of London.

HARRIET AND ELIZA

Registered 30 December 1858; Joseph Gosterlow, Master and part-owner.

Schooner, carvel built, standing bowsprit, length overall 65' 8/10, beam 17' 8/10, depth 8' 2/10 = 61 tons.

Part-owner Henry Walker; registered No. 25187.

14 November 1875, lost at sea in the North Sea WNW of Lowestoft a distance about 50 miles. The crew, landed at Ramsgate and had lost everything.

HERALD

Registered, 18 January 1859; John Chester, Master & owner.

Schooner, carvel built. length overall 62' 8/10, beam 18' 4/10, depth 9' 3/10 = 69 tons.

Registered No. 258.

1867, owners John Chester and Clement Sharman.

19 November 1875, sailed from Newcastle bound for the Isle of Wight and has not been heard of since. Registration Certificate lost with the vessel.

FRIENDS

15 February 1860.

Sloop, topping up bowsprit, length overall 56' 2/10, beam 15', depth 6' = 34 tons.

Owner Isaac Greenhall.

18 March 1873, owner, Thomas Walker.

27 March 1873, registration transferred to Kingston upon Hull.

MARY ANN

Built 1831.

Sloop, clincher built, length overall 56' 8/10, beam 14', depth 6' = 56 tons.

Thomas Royce, owner.

20 November 1867, Thomas Royce sold 64 shares to Matthew Southwell Vine.

Registration cancelled 24 December 1867.

ANNIE

Built 1842.

Sloop, carvel and Clincher built, length overall 57' 4/10, beam 15' 9/10,
    depth 5' 7/10 = 41 tons.

John Hayes of Spalding.

1863, vessel lost.

LONDON PACKET

Built at Wells, Norfolk, 1812.

Brigantine,[1] carvel built, length overall 67' 8/10, beam 19' 1/10, depth 10' 1/10
    = 81 tons.

4 February 1862, owner, Matthew S. Vine.

8 December 1862, sold to George Smeed, Theophilous Smith & William
    Samuel Harris.

SYLPH

Registered 22 May 1861, Boston; built at Auderton, Cornwall, 1849.

Three-mast schooner, carvel built, length overall 64' 6/10, beam 13' 9/10,
    depth, 8' 3/10 = 32 tons.

Owner, Henry Bugg, registered No. 8537.

5 May 1874, sold to George Wadham.

12 May 1874, re-registered at Cowes, Isle of Wight, under name *Serena*.

SAMUEL

Built 1849.

Sloop, clincher built, length overall 57' 5/10, beam 14' 6/10, depth 5' 7/10
    = 34 tons.

13 November 1862, owner, James Atkin,

29 June 1876, sold to Henry Batty of Hull.

---

1 A brigantine is a vessel with two masts rigged with square sails on the foremast and
   fore-and-aft sails rigged on the mainmast.

WSR

Built at Kingston upon Hull, 1845.

Sloop, clincher & carvel built, length overall 58' 8/10, beam 15' 5/10, depth 7' = 42 tons.

4 February 1863, owner, Samuel Culpin.

25 January 1869, owner, George Levesley.

19 April 1872, owner, Joseph Dunn.

HOPE

Built at Wakefield, Yorkshire, 1829.

Sloop, carvel & clincher built. Length overall 56' 9/10, Beam 15' 3/10, Depth 6' 2/10 = 35 tons.

27 March 1863, owner, Edward Royce of Albert Street, Spalding.

29 March 1877, sold to John Doads & John Toplady of Hull.

BREEZE

Built at Kingston upon Hull, 1845.

Schooner, carvel built, length overall 62' 5/10, beam 15' 9/10, depth 7' 5/10 = 54 tons.

Registration No. 19698.

27 May 1863, owner, William Green of Spalding,

1868, lost at sea.

MARY CATHERINE

Built 1840.

Ketch, carvel & clincher built, length overall 59' 5/10, beam 15' 7/10, depth 6' 7/10 = 45 tons.

4 March 1864, John Hayes, owner.

13 March 1891, Robert Arthur & John William Hayes, owners.

3 May 1895, certificate delivered up at Kingston upon Hull.

HENRIETTA

Built at Garnmouth, Moray, 1847.

Schooner, carvel built, length overall 64' 5/10, beam 19' 2/10, depth 9' 2/10 = 70 tons.

6 November 1864, owner, William Wright, died intestate 5 January 1867.

21 February 1868, sold to William Sewell of Spalding.

June 1869, lost at sea.

EDWARD

Built at Barnby Bridge, Sheffield Canal, 18 August 1850.

Sloop, clincher built, length overall 55' 4/10, beam 14' 5/10, depth 6' 3/10 = 35 tons.

9 January 1865, owner Henry Walker of Spalding.

23 May 1870, owner Robert Payne.

22 May 1880, sold to Samuel Hull of Kingston upon Hull.

GERM

Built at Leverington, Cambridgeshire, 13 June 1864.

Ketch, carvel built, length overall 75', beam 19', depth 9' 2/10, = 72 49/100 tons.

24 April 1866, Henry Walker, owner. Henry died 20 September 1873 and the vessel was sold to Robert Dannatt of Barrow on Humber, Lincolnshire, 29 October 1873.

BETA

Built at Sunderland, 1860.

Schooner, carvel built, length overall 76', beam 19' 5/10, depth 9' 7/10 = 89 14/100 tons.

Registration No. 28316.

10 August 1866, John Chester of Albert Street, Spalding, owner.

13 November 1873, sold to Henry Walker and William Thomas Capps.

2 November 1890, lost at sea off Goatness Point.

MARY ANN

Built at Methley, Yorkshire, 1831.

Sloop, clincher built, length overall 56' 8/10, beam 14' 6/10, depth 6' = 32 61/100 tons.

24 December 1867, owner Matthew Southwell Vine.

5 June 1875, sold to Joseph Harrison & Robert Donnison.

2 August 1882, wrecked on the Roaring Middle, Boston Deeps.

LAUREL

Built at Doncaster, Yorkshire, 1838.

Sloop, length overall 56' 6/10, beam 14' 8/10, depth 6' = 34 55/100 tons

27 March 1868, Thomas Royce of Spalding, owner. Thomas died 9 November 1878, vessel transferred to Harriet Royce, John Turner & Charles Bower.

22 June 1898, sold to George Francis Birch.

November 1906, broken up.

HOLBEACH

Built at Boston, 1878.

Sloop, carvel built, length overall 57' 9/10, beam 16', depth 5' 4/10 = 38 31/100 tons.

3 January 1879, owner Joseph Caudwell (farmer).

22 May 1888, foundered off Guernsey.

The Sloop *Walcot* was built by
John Wray in 1854 for Mr Thomas
Spilman and Mr John Barley of
Whitton, for the sum of £380.
Billy-boys like the *Walcot* were
still clincher-built (with the hull
cladding overlapping) up to the
end of the nineteenth century, and
they were the largest vessel of this
type of construction in Europe. They
were constructed with elm keels
and strong oak frames, knees and
cladding, with pine decking on oak
cross beams and the cargo hold
lined with pine boards. (Photograph
reproduced by kind permission of
Mr Tom Smith of Whitton)

The *Lizzie & Annie* in Hull Docks.
(Mrs Margaret Johnson collection)

7

CENSUSES AND DIRECTORIES

1841 Census, Spalding

Name	Occupation	Address
Richard Glenn	Fisherman	Mill House Marsh
Elizabeth Thompson	Wife of Mariner at Sea (John)	Pigeon End
John Grantham	Mariner	Pigeon End
Ann Levesley	Wife of Mariner at Sea (William Fredrick)	Pigeon End
Charlotte Neal	Wife of Mariner at Sea	Pigeon End
James Glenn	Mariner	Pigeon End
John Johnson	Mariner	Pigeon End
Joseph Woodward	Mariner	Pigeon End
Eliza Wilson	Wife of Mariner at Sea (Benjamin)	Pigeon End
John Cope	Pilot	Pigeon End
Sarah Wilkinson	Wife of Mariner at Sea (Henry)	Pigeon End
Susan Wilkinson	Wife of Mariner at Sea (Richard)	Pigeon End
Nathaniel Boon	Fisherman	Pigeon End
John Beard	Mariner	Pigeon End
William Glenn	Fisherman	Pigeon End
Thomas Glenn	Fisherman	Pigeon End
Eleanor Enderby	Wife of Mariner at Sea (John Fisher)	Commercial Road
James Wright	Mariner	Commercial Road
William White	Mariner	Commercial Road
Henry Bran	Mariner	Commercial Road

Michael Wilkinson	Mariner	Commercial Road
William Atkinson	Mariner	Commercial Road
Auden Smith	Mariner	Commercial Road
Matthew Kellan	Sailor	Commercial Road
George Booth	Marine	Commercial Road
Thomas Wilkinson	Pilot	Commercial Road
Catherine Green	Wife of Mariner at Sea (William Robertson)	Commercial Road
John Seaton	Mariner	Commercial Road
John Kirk	Mariner	Commercial Road
William Burgham	Mariner	Commercial Road
Joseph Dunn	Mariner	Commercial Road
Matthew Vine	Mariner	Commercial Road
Edward Jackson	Mariner	Commercial Road
James Audlin	Mariner	Commercial Road
Thomas Audlin	Mariner	Commercial Road
William Sharp	Waterman	Commercial Road
John Willcox	Mariner	Commercial Road
Thomas Rosbe	Ship Owner	Commercial Road
William Royce	Fisherman	Commercial Road
Mary Johnson	Wife of Mariner at Sea (John or Richard)	Commercial Road
Eliza Jackson	Wife of Mariner at Sea (Edward Robert)	Commercial Road
Martha Booth	Wife of Mariner at Sea	Commercial Road
Zacharia Day	Fisherman	Commercial Road
James Clarke	Mariner	Commercial Road
Thomas Royce	Fisherman	Commercial Road
Elizabeth Cope	Wife of Mariner at Sea (John)	Commercial Road
Mary Winfield	Wife of Mariner at Sea (William)	Commercial Road
Sarah Boyce	Wife of Mariner at Sea (John)	Commercial Road
John Smith	Boatman	Commercial Road
William Collins	Mariner	Commercial Road
John Collins	Pilot	Commercial Road
Isaac Brothwell	Boatman	Gas House Lane
William Penneston	Boatman	Gas House Lane

George Wingfield	Mariner	Gas House Lane
John Perch	Mariner	Gas House Lane
John Willis	Mariner	Gas House Lane
James Rogerson	Mariner	Gas House Lane
John Carter	Mariner	Albion Street
William Green	Mariner	Albion Street
John Austwick	Mariner	Albion Street
James Tupman	Mariner	Albion Street
Richard Blessed	Waterman	Westlode Street

Master Mariners of Spalding, *White's Directory* 1842

Name	Occupation	Address
John Booth	Master Mariner	Holbeach Road
John Boyce	Master Mariner	Holbeach Road
James Clark	Master Mariner	Holbeach Road
John Hayes	Master Mariner	Holbeach Road
John Johnson	Master Mariner	Holbeach Road
Richard Johnson	Master Mariner	Holbeach Road
John Kirk	Master Mariner	Holbeach Road
John Seymour	Master Mariner	Holbeach Road
Arden Smith	Master Mariner	Holbeach Road
Benjamin Ward	Master Mariner	Holbeach Road
John White	Master Mariner	Holbeach Road
William White	Master Mariner	Holbeach Road
Benjamin Wilson	Master Mariner	Holbeach Road
Charles Wilkinson	Master Mariner	Holbeach Road
Richard Wilkinson	Master Mariner	Holbeach Road
Richard Carter	Vessel Owner	Albion Street
William Burton	Master Mariner	Albion Street
Thomas Draper	Master Mariner	Albion Street
James Tupman	Master Mariner	Albion Street
John Pannell	Boat Builder	Albion Street
Thomas Perch	Master Mariner	Marsh Lane
Samuel Platt	Master Mariner	Marsh Lane
Richard Culpin	Master Mariner	Double Street

A sketch map showing the area close to the river where many of the Spalding mariners lived.

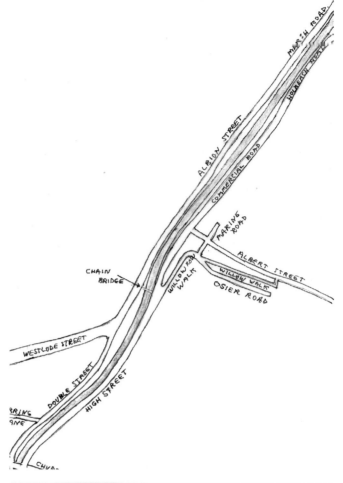

The backs of the cottages on Commercial Road next to the River Welland. (F. Parkinson, Spalding Gentlemen's Society collection)

A view upstream showing Albion Street with Pannell's boatyard on the right. (F. Parkinson, Spalding Gentlemen's Society collection)

Master Mariners of Spalding, *Slater's Directory* 1849

Name	Address
Thomas Draper jnr	Albion Street
William Ellis	Albion Street
J. Woodward	Albion Street

Master Mariners of Spalding, *White's Directory* 1856

Name	Address
Samuel Atkin	Commercial Road
Joseph Pakey	Commercial Road
John Chester	Albert Place
Richard Culpin Snr	Holbeach Road
Richard Culpin jnr	Holbeach Road
William Crooks	Holbeach Road

John Knott	Holbeach Road
Thomas Royce	Holbeach Road
William Storr	Holbeach Road
Henry Wilkinson	Holbeach Road
Joseph Woodward	Holbeach Road
Thomas Draper Snr	Albion Street
Joseph Dunn	Albion Street
William Green	Albion Street
Joseph Gosterlow	Albion Street
Edward Todd Richardson	Albion Street
John Greenhall	Albert Street
Isaac Greenhall	Albert Street
John Hayes	Albert Street
Edward Jackson	Albert Street
George Levesley	Albert Street
John Taylor	Willow Row Walk
Matthew Vine	Willow Row Walk

Vessels and Master Mariners, 1850–52 and 1859–67

From entries in the two ledgers of Edward Fisher, blacksmith, in the possession of Geoff Dodd, the last owner of the Chain Bridge Forge:

Vessel	Name	Type	Date	Details
Ancholme	Capt. Isacc Greenhall	Sloop		
Anne	Capt. J. Hayes jnr		1860–61	
Ann and Maria	Capt. J. Jackson	Sloop	1850–52	
Aurora	Capt. Joseph Pakey	Sloop	1860–65	
Breeze	Capt. George Levesley	Sloop	1850–52	Living at 22 Willow Walk, Spalding
Breeze	Capt. Matthew Southwell Vine	Sloop	1860–64	Living at 27 Willow Row, Spalding

David and Ann	Capt. Henry Wilkinson	Sloop	1850	Living at Holbeach Road, Spalding
David and Ann	Mrs Wilkinson, Owner		1850–51	
Diligent	Owner of	Sloop	1850	
Edward	Capt. E. Payne	Sloop	1865–66	
Ellen	Capt. Matthew Southwell Vine	Sloop	1851	
Elizabeth	Capt. Jackson	Sloop	1851	
Elizabeth	Capt. Joseph Atkin	Sloop	1860	Living at 13 Marsh Road, Spalding
Freedom	Capt. Wright	Sloop	1861–64	
Freedom	Capt. William Dunn	Sloop	1865–66	
Friends	Capt. Isaac Greenhall	Sloop	1860–62	
George and Susan	Capt. William Storr	Sloop	1856	Living at Holbeach Road, Spalding
Glen	Owner of	Sloop	1850–52 and 1862	
Hero	Capt. White	Sloop	1865	
Hope	Capt. Samuel Culpin	Sloop	1860–62	
Hope	Capt. Edward Royce	Sloop	1863–66	
Jane	Capt. Colley	Sloop	1850–51	
Joseph and Ann	Owner, Mr G. Sly		1850–51 and 1861–64	
Laurel	Capt. William Green	Sloop	1856	Living at Holbeach Road, Spalding
Lucy Ellen	Capt. Neal	Sloop		
Margaret	Capt. E. Jackson	Sloop	1856	Living at Albert Street, Spalding
Maria	Capt. J. Gosterlow	Sloop		Living at 41 Commercial Road, Spalding
Martha	Capt. J. Harrison	Sloop	1850	
Mary	Capt. Isaac Greenhall	Sloop	1856	

Mary Ann	Capt. S. Culpin	Sloop	1850–52	Living at Holbeach Road, Spalding
Mary Ann	Capt. T. Royce		1860–66	
Mary I Marsden	Owner of	Sloop	1850–52	
Mary I Marsden	Capt. Robert Payne	Sloop	1859–64	
Medcalf	Owner of	Sloop	1850–52	
Medcalf	Capt. J. Pakey	Sloop	1860–61	
Melita	Capt. John Hayes Snr	Sloop	1850–52 and 1860–63	Living at Albert Street, Spalding
Ocean	Capt. Joseph Gosterlow	Sloop	1850–52	Living at Holbeach Road, Spalding
Providence	Capt. J. Taylor	Sloop	1850–52	Living at Willow Row Walk, Spalding
Providence	Capt. Ellis	Sloop	1860	
Red Rover	Mr Henry Bugg	Yacht	1860–66	
Samuel	Capt. James Atkin	Sloop	1860–64	
Samuel Barnard	Capt. Joseph Vine	Schooner	1861–63	
Sarah	Owner of	Sloop	1850	
Sarah	Capt. Edward Jackson	Sloop	1860–61	
Sarah	Capt. J. Turner	Sloop	1862–66	
Sea	Capt. E. Robinson		1850–52	
	Mr T. Draper, Owner			
Sea	Capt. John Greenhall	Sloop	1856	Living at Albert Street, Spalding. Lost at sea, 20 May 1860
Sisters	Capt. William Ellis	Sloop	1851	
2 Sisters	Capt. Joseph Pakey	Sloop	1850–52	Living at Commercial Road, Spalding
Truefriend	Capt. Colley	Sloop	1851	
Urania	Owners of	Sloop	1851	

Violet	Capt. Joseph Dunn	Sloop	1860–65	Living at 1 Holbeach Road, Spalding
Victoria	Capt. Hollis	Smack	1864	Fosdyke
Wellington	Capt. E. Robinson	Sloop	1850	
Wellington	Capt. James Atkin	Sloop	1860	
W R S	Owner of		1850–52	
W R S	Capt. S. Culpin	Sloop	1862–65	

1851 Census, Spalding

Name	Occupation	Address
Thomas Royce	Mariner	Albion Place
Anne Draper	Wife of Mariner	Albion Street
James Rogerson	Retired Mariner	Albion Street
George Pidd	Mariner	Albion Street
George Wingfield	Mariner	Albion Street
Thomas Draper	Ship Owner	Albion Street
Mary Richardson	Wife of Mariner (Edward Todd)	Albion Street
Thomas Sawyer	Mariner	Marsh Rails
William Royce	Fisherman	Holbeach Road
Thomas Royce	Mariner	Holbeach Road
Joseph Royce	Fisherman	Holbeach Road
Richard Culpin	Master Mariner	Holbeach Road
Catherine Green	Mariner's Wife (William Robertson)	Holbeach Road
Thomas Wilkinson	Mariner	Holbeach Road
John Cope	Fisherman	Holbeach Road
George Nightingale	Sailor	Holbeach Road
Joseph Gostelow	Master Mariner	Holbeach Road
Ann Wright	Mariner's Wife (Joseph)	Holbeach Road
Eleanor Enderby	Mariner's Wife (John)	Holbeach Road
Richard Wilkinson	Sailor	Holbeach Road
William White	Harbour Master	Holbeach Road
Fredrick Levesley	Sailor	Holbeach Road
Edward Johnson	Sailor	Holbeach Road

Isaac Gosterlow	Mariner	Holbeach Road
James Munton	Boatman	Holbeach Road
Thomas G. Glenn	Fisherman	Holbeach Road
Elizabeth Pakey	Mariner's Wife (John)	Albert Street
Rebecca Turner	Sailor's Wife (Edward Henry)	Albert Street
Mary Atkin	Mariner's Wife (Joseph)	Albert Street
George E. Hugh	Sailor	Albert Street
Hannah Vine	Mariner's Wife (Matthew Southwell)	Willow Row
William Patton	Mariner	Willow Row
Sarah Jackson	Sea Captain's Wife (Edward)	
James Stephenson	Mariner	Behind Holbeach Road

A sloop unloading via a gangplank to the High Street. (F. Parkinson, Spalding Gentlemen's Society collection)

Empty barges next to the High Street at low tide. Note the small crane and timber, which are possibly for George Burdett, timber merchant. (F. Parkinson, Spalding Gentlemen's Society collection)

Merchant Marine Census

The enumeration of the merchant marine was not done on one day but was spread over a period of time.

No schedules appear to have been issued in 1841 and very few of the 1851 shipping schedules have survived.

In 1861 a ship's schedule was given by the customs officers to the Master of every British foreign-going home-trade and coasting ship or vessel in port on 25 March or which arrived between that day and census day, 7 April. These to be returned on arrival in port between 8 April and 7 May. In 1871 the schedules were issued from 25 March until census day 2 April and were to be collected in port from 3 April to 2 May. In 1881 they were issued from 26 March to census day 3 April and were to be collected between 4 April and 3 May. In 1891 they were issued on 30 March ready for census day on 5 April and collected on arrival in port between 6 April and 30 June.

On the front of the schedule the master filled in the following information: name of the vessel official number (if any) port or place to which it belonged, tonnage description and trade in which it was employed, name of master, place at which the schedule was delivered to the master, the date of delivery and the position of the vessel at midnight on the day of the census. In 1891 for the first time they had to state whether the vessel was sail or steam powered.

On the inside the following information was to be provided: the names of the master and crew, married or unmarried, male or female, age at last birthday, rank, profession or occupation, and where they were born.

If a ship or coasting vessel arrived in port after the census day, the master was to be asked if he had handed in his census to any UK port. If not, he was requested to fill up a ship's schedule and hand it in to the customs officer.

Merchant Marine Census, 1861

Vessel	Master	Type	Tonnage	Where Registered	Position at Time of Census
Anne	John Hayes jnr	Sloop	41 tons	Registered Boston	Middlesbrough
Aurora	Richard Wright	Sloop	50 tons	Registered Boston	Between the head of the Humber
Breeze	William Green	Schooner	54 tons	Registered Hull	Flamborough Head, North-West 8 miles
Breeze	Matthew Vine	Sloop	57 tons	Registered Boston	Caen
Eagle	William Platton	Sloop	39 tons	Registered Boston	Goole Dock
Elizabeth	Joseph Atkin	Sloop	33 tons	Registered Boston	Sutton Wash
Favourite	Fredrick Bland	Keel	15 tons	Registered Boston	Employed upon the Welland outfall works, moored near Fosdyke Bridge
Friends	Isaac Greenhall	Coasting Barge	40 tons	Port of Spalding	In the Medway, Kent
Glen	John Hubbard	Sloop	49 tons	Registered Boston	At anchor in sea reach

George and Susannah	William Storr	Coasting barge	21 tons	Registered Boston	Holbeach Creek
Hope	Alfred Craley	Sloop	36 tons	Registered Hull	Wootten Harbour, Norfolk
Hope	Samuel Culpin	Sloop	35 tons	Registered Goole	Off Flamborough Head
Joseph and Ann	George Levesley	Sloop	34 tons	Registered Boston	Riding at anchor, Boston Deeps
Laurel	William Green	Sloop	40 tons	Registered Boston	Blacktoft Roads
Mary Ann	Joseph Royce	Sloop	43 tons	Registered Goole	Broadfleet Sands
Mary Ann	Thomas Royce	Sloop	32 tons	Registered Boston	Moored at Fosdyke Bridge, River Welland
Mary and S. Marsden	John Knott	Sloop	39 tons	Port of Spalding	Resting in Hawk Roads
Melita	John Hayes	Schooner	40 tons	Registered Boston	Middlesbrough Dock
Metcalf	Joseph Pakey	Sloop	38 tons	Registered Boston	Whitby
Providence	William Ellis	Sloop	32 tons	Registered Boston	Wootten, Norfolk
Providence	W. Thompson	Sloop	49 tons	Registered Goole	Off Cromer
Sarah	Edward Jackson	Schooner	37 tons	Registered Boston	Anchored in Clayhole, Boston
Samuel Barnard	Joseph Vine	Schooner	60 tons	Registered Boston	At Sea[1]
Violet	Joseph Dunn	Sloop	31 tons	Registered Boston	Moored at Spalding

1 Samuel Barnard was a radical blue-party Boston man with links to Liquorpond Street and Blue Street in Boston, residences of many ships' captains in the 1800s.

William	Henry Jarvis, 51, born Spalding, Mate	Coasting Ketch	48 tons	Registered Yarmouth	At Penzance
Zoe	Clement Sharman	Schooner	74 tons	Registered Hull	Queen's Dock, Hull
No name	Beasley Pepper	Lighter, Inland Navigation	14 tons	Registered Boston	Moored at Deeping St James[2]

Crew Born Spalding and District, 1861 Census

Name	Position	Age	Where Born
John Chatterton	Boy	16	Spalding
Isaac Chambers	Boy	16	Spalding
Albert Cocking	Mate	21	Spalding
Richard Culpin	Seaman		Spalding
William Culpin	Boy	18	Spalding
Henry Day	Mate	19	Spalding
John Dunn	Boy	14	Spalding
Joseph Dunn	Cook	14	Spalding
Thomas Dunn	Seaman	18	Spalding
William Dunn	Mate	52	Spalding
John Enderby	Mate	29	Spalding
John Enderby	Mate	53	Spalding
William Enderby	Mate	25	Spalding
Robert Hayes	Mate	22	Spalding
William Hayes	Boy	17	Spalding
George Gaunt	Mate	31	Spalding
Robert Geant	Seaman	24	Spalding
William Green	Mate	25	Spalding
John Jinks	Seaman	23	Spalding

---

1   This last one shows that some goods were still being transported by river at least as far as the Deepings in 1861. The census form had been issued to the Master on 4 April at Fosdyke.

Henry Knott	Boy	16	Spalding
Robert Laythorpe	Mate	25	Spalding
Richard Nop	Seaman	20	Spalding
George Pidd	Boy	16	Spalding
John Pepper	Seaman	15	Spalding
George Platton	Seaman	16	Spalding
William Rooksley	Mate	20	Spalding
Edward Royce	Mate	24	Spalding
William South	Mate	38	Spalding
John Henry Vine	Boy	16	Spalding
Edward Ward	Boy	16	Spalding
Richard Wilkinson	Mate	27	Spalding
William Scott	Seaman	18	Long Sutton
Henry Brown	Seaman	19	Western
Joseph Kitchen	Mate	28	Western

1861 Census, Spalding

Name	Occupation	Address
Bridget Pakey	Wife of Merchant Sailor at Sea (Joseph)	High Street
William Cope	Fisherman	Holbeach Road
Zachariah Day	Fisherman	Holbeach Road
Thomas Rice	Fisherman	Holbeach Road
William Royce	Fisherman	Holbeach Road
James T. Wells	Fisherman	Holbeach Road
Joseph Royce	Fisherman	Holbeach Road
William Davis	Merchant Seaman	Holbeach Road
George Booth	Retired Merchant Seaman	Holbeach Road
Richard Culpin	Merchant Seaman	Holbeach Road
Harriet Royce	Wife of Merchant Seaman at Sea (Thomas)	Holbeach Road
Elizabeth Collins	Wife of Merchant Seaman at Sea (William)	Holbeach Road
Elizabeth Green	Wife of Merchant Seaman at Sea (William)	Holbeach Road
William Royce	Merchant Seaman	Holbeach Road

Mary Pidd	Wife of Merchant Seaman at Sea (George)	Holbeach Road
Joseph Dunn	Merchant Seaman	Holbeach Road
Ellen Enderby	Wife of Merchant Seaman at Sea (John)	Holbeach Road
James Chandler	Formerly Merchant Seaman	Holbeach Road
Mary Vine	Wife of Merchant Seaman at Sea (Joseph)	Holbeach Road
Rebecca Woodward	Wife of Merchant Seaman at Sea (Joseph)	Holbeach Road
Hannah Levesley	Wife of Merchant Seaman at Sea	Holbeach Road
William White	Harbour Master	Holbeach Road
Mary A. Warby	Wife of Merchant Seaman at Sea	Holbeach Road
William Taylor	Boatman	Holbeach Road
Elizabeth Jarvis	Wife of Merchant Seaman at Sea (Henry)	Holbeach Road
Robert Wilson	Fisherman	Marsh Road
James Munton	Fisherman	Marsh Road
Sarah Sharman	Wife of Merchant Seaman at Sea (Clement)	Albert Street
Elizabeth Hayes	Wife of Merchant Seaman at Sea (John)	Albert Street
Samuel Cope	Fisherman	Albert Street
Susannah Royce	Wife of Merchant Seaman at Sea (Thomas)	Albert Street
John Cullum	Merchant Seaman	Albert Street
Sarah Jackson	Wife of Merchant Seaman at Sea (Edward)	Albert Street
Sarah Chester	Wife of Merchant Seaman at Sea (John)	Albert Street
Eliza Gostelow	Wife of Merchant Seaman at Sea (Joseph)	Albert Street
Ann Culpin	Wife of Merchant Seaman at Sea (Samuel)	Willow Row
Eliza Knott	Wife of Merchant Seaman at Sea (John)	Willow Row
Eliza Platton	Wife of Merchant Seaman at Sea (William)	Willow Row
Hannah Vine	Wife of Merchant Seaman at Sea (Matthew Southwell)	Willow Row
George Levesley	Merchant Seaman	Willow Row
John Thompson	Formerly Merchant Seaman	Back Lane

Mary Ann Atkin	Wife of Merchant Seaman at Sea (Joseph)	Marsh Rail Road
James Atkin	Master Mariner	Marsh Rail Road
Thomas Brothwell	Mariner	Marsh Rail Road
Thomas Smith	Mariner	Marsh Rail Road
Thomas Draper	Retired Master Mariner	Albion Street
Ann Conningworth	Mariner's Wife (Richard Robert)	Albion Street
Richard Todd Richardson	Mariner	Albion Street

1862 Census

Vessel	Master	Type	Tonnage	Position at Time of Census
Freedom	William Dunn			Spalding
Hope	E. Royce	Sloop	35 tons	Spalding
Sarah	John Turner	Sloop		Commercial Road

Master Mariners of Spalding, *Post Office Directory* 1868

Name	Occupation	Address
George Levesley	Master Mariner	Willow Row Walk
Edward Richardson	Master Mariner and Ship Owner	Albion Street
Matthew Vine	Ship Owner	Commercial Road

Merchant Marine Census, 1871

Vessel	Master and Crew	Type	Tonnage	Where Registered	Position at Time of Census
Beta	John Chester, Master	Schooner	89 tons	Registered Boston	At Plymouth
Ebenezer	James Boon, Master	Sloop	38 tons	Registered Hull	At Queens Dock, Hull

	Mary Ann Boon, Master's Wife				
Friends	William Royce, Master	Sloop	35 tons	Registered Boston	At Boston, Skirbeck Quarter.
	Richard Knott, Mate				
Hartlepool	Joseph Wilkinson, Mate	Coasting Brigg	208 tons	Registered Sunderland	Off Woolwich, River Thames
Herald	Clement Sharman, Master		69 tons	Registered Boston	At Rochester
	Walter Scott, Mate				
	Robert William Parker, Ordinary Sailor born Boston				
	Sarah Sharman, Master's Wife				
Laurel	William Royce jnr, Master	Sloop	34 tons	Registered Boston	Canal, Castleford, Yorkshire
	James Thompson, Mate, born Deeping				
	Ann Royce, Master's Wife				
Olive	Robert Atkin, Mate	Billy-boy schooner	35 tons	Registered Goole	Crossing Kent
Rapid	Henry Knott, Master	Schooner	57 tons	Registered Boston	At anchor, Grays Reach, River Thames
	Joseph Lewis, Mate				
	William Knott, Seaman				

Samuel	James Atkin, Master	Sloop	34 tons	Registered Boston	Moored in Goole Canal
	Alfred Stoleman, Mate				
	William Atkin, Seaman				
Sarah	John Turner, Master	Sloop	40 tons	Registered Boston	At Snettisham Beech Norfolk
	William Enderby, Mate				

1871 Census, Spalding

Name	Occupation	Address
Biddy Pakey	Wife of Mariner at Sea (Joseph)	High Street
Rebecca A. Vine	Wife of Mariner at Sea (John Henry)	High Street
Thomas Royce	Fisherman	Holbeach Road
Joseph Royce	Fisherman	Holbeach Road
Ann Ewen	Wife of Sailor at Sea	Holbeach Road
Zachariah Day	Fisherman	Holbeach Road
George Pidd	Mariner	Holbeach Road
John L. Ward	Sailor	Holbeach Road
James M. Munton	Fisherman	Holbeach Road
John Munton	Sailor	Holbeach Road
William Dale	Boatman	Holbeach Road
Mary Vine	Wife of Mariner at Sea (Joseph)	Holbeach Road
John Wilson	Boat Hauler (Barge Waterman)	Holbeach Road
Richard Culpin	Mariner	Holbeach Road
Martha Burton	Wife of Mariner at Sea (Samuel)	Holbeach Road
Rebecca Atkin	Wife of Mariner at Sea	Holbeach Road
William Horton	Mariner	Holbeach Road
Ann Turner	Wife of Master Mariner at Sea (John)	Holbeach Road
Elizabeth Stedman	Wife of Mariner at Sea	Holbeach Road
Joseph Dunn	Master Mariner	Holbeach Road

William Dunn	Mariner	Holbeach Road
Stephen Dunn	Mariner	Holbeach Road
Thomas Dunn	Mariner	Holbeach Road
Elizabeth Vine	Wife of Mariner at Sea (Joseph)	Holbeach Road
Rebecca Woodward	Wife of Mariner at Sea (Joseph)	Holbeach Road
Joseph Lewis	Boatman	Holbeach Road
Thomas Smith	Boatman	Holbeach Road
Elizabeth Royce	Wife of Master Mariner at Sea (Edward)	Albert Street
Ann Jones	Wife of Master Mariner at Sea (William)	Albert Street
Hannah Levesley	Wife of Mariner at Sea	Albert Street
Thomas Stedman	Harbour Master	Albert Street
John Cullum	Mariner	Albert Street
John Sketcher	Mariner	Albert Street
Sarah Wright	Wife of Mariner at Sea (Richard)	Albert Street
Joseph Gosterlow	Mariner	Albert Street
Edward Todd Richardson	Formerly Master Mariner	Harveys New Road
Mark Depear	Mariner	Back Lane
Eliza Hayes	Wife of Mariner at Sea (John)	Back Lane
Eliza Platton	Formerly Mariner's Wife	Willow Row Walk
George Levesley	Master Mariner	Willow Row Walk

1872 Census

Vessel	Master	Type	Position at Time of Census
Edward	R. Payne	Sloop	Holbeach Road
Medcalf	Joseph Pakey	Sloop	High Street

Master Mariners of Spalding, *White's Directory* 1872

Name	Occupation	Address
Joseph Atkin	Master Mariner	Marsh Road
Joseph Dunn	Master Mariner	Holbeach Road

Robert Payne	Master Mariner	Holbeach Road
George Sly	Ship Owner	Holbeach Road
Joseph Woodward	Master Mariner	Holbeach Road
Samuel Atkin	Master Mariner	Commercial Road
Joseph Binks	Master Mariner	Commercial Road
Clement Sharman	Master Mariner	Commercial Road
John Turner	Master Mariner	Commercial Road
Joseph Gosterlow	Ship Owner and Master Mariner	Commercial Road
Joseph Vine	Master Mariner	Commercial Road
Adam Westmoreland	Ship's Mate	Commercial Road
John Chester	Ship Owner and Master Mariner	Albert Street
John Hayes	Master Mariner	Albert Street
Edward Richardson	Ship Owner	Albert Street
Richard Wright	Master Mariner	Albert Street
George Levesley	Master Mariner	Willow Walk
Matthew Vine	Ship Owner	Willow Walk
Joseph Pakey	Master Mariner	High Street
John Henry Vine	Master Mariner	High Street

From Other Census Returns and Directories of Spalding
1881–95

Vessel	Crew	Type	Tonnage	Where Registered	Location and Date
Artos	Robert Atkin, 1st Officer	Screw Steamer	1,174 tons	Registered Hull	Dunkerque, France, 1881
Beta	John Chester	Schooner	89 tons	Registered Boston	Durham, 1881
Fern	Harry England	Sailing Keel	80 tons	Registered Hull	Old Harbour Hull, 1891
John	James Charles Atkin	Sloop	47 tons	Registered Lynn	Hull Harbour, 1881
	Charles Atkin, Mate				
John and Elizabeth	Thomas Dunn	Sailing	50 ton	Registered Goole	Moored at Hunts Works, 1891

Leo X111	Joseph Vine	Schooner	77 tons	Registered Newcastle	Town Quay, Southampton, 1881
Mary Jane	Joseph Gosterlow				Lost at Sea, 1895
Roarer	Thomas Royce			Lost at Sea	
Samuel	James Atkin	Sloop		Spalding	
Sarah	R. Duckering	Ketch	56 tons	Registered Goole	River Thames, Limehouse, 1891
William Royce	Thomas Royce				

1881 Census, Spalding

Name	Occupation	Address
Joseph Atkin	Harbour Master	Marsh Road
Thomas Tomlinson	Mariner's Mate	Marsh Road
William Bowman	Ordinary Seaman	Marsh Road
Joseph Dunn	Mariner	Holbeach Road
Joseph Lewis	Mariner	Holbeach Road
John Cullum	Mariner	Albert Street
Edward Royce	Mariner	Albert Street
William Dale	Sailor	Commercial Road
Joseph Gosterlow	Retired Mariner	Commercial Road
Joseph Kitchen	Sailor	Commercial Road
James Laythorpe	Sailor	Commercial Road
Robert Peacock	Sailor	Commercial Road
John Rooksby	Mariner	Commercial Road
William Royce	Mariner	Commercial Road
Alfred Stolham	Mariner	Commercial Road
John Turner	Master Mariner	Commercial Road
Edward Ward	Mariner	Commercial Road
George Levesley	Master Mariner	Willow Walk
John Henry Vine	Master Mariner	High Street

Joseph Lewis	Mariner	New Road
John Seaton	Retired Sailor	Double Street
William Dunn	Master Mariner	Double Street

Kelly's Directory 1885

Name	Occupation	Address
James Atkin	Master Mariner	Albion Street
Joseph Atkin	Master Mariner	Marsh Road
Smith Edwards Dring	Boat Builder	Marsh Road
John Pannell	Boat Builder	Marsh Rail Road
Joseph Dunn	Master Mariner	Holbeach Road
George Levesley	Master Mariner	Willow Row Walk
Edward Royce	Master Mariner	Albert Street
Joseph Royce	Master Mariner	Albert Street
John Turner	Master Mariner	Commercial Road
Joseph Vine	Master Mariner	Commercial Road
Adam Westmoreland	Ship's Mate	Commercial Road
John Henry Vine	Master Mariner	High Street

Kelly's Directory 1889

Name	Occupation	Address
Joseph Atkin	Master Mariner	Marsh Road
Joseph Pannell	Boat Builder	Marsh Road
Smith Edwards Dring	Boat Builder	Marsh Road
John Richard Grassam	Master Mariner	Albert Street
James Levesley	Master Mariner	Willow Walk
George Levesley	Master Mariner	(Marine Ville) Willow Walk

Decline

Shipping on the Welland was in decline towards the end of the 1880s. The railway had reached Spalding in 1848 and had cast a gloom over the mariners and those engaged in the river traffic. The railway company wanted to put a bridge over the river for the Spalding to Holbeach line at Fulney, but the mariners opposed the scheme thinking a bridge there would interfere with the river traffic, and eventually the company had to build it between London Road and Cowbit Road, much further upstream of the town.

The following will give an idea how the railways affected the shipping in the Welland:

> By an Act of 1824 the drainage of these districts was entrusted to a body called 'The General Works Trustees', constituted in lieu of the old commissioners. This body had the power to levy drainage taxes upon about 24,000 acres, and also to receive dues on vessels navigating the River Welland. This latter source of income diminished considerably upon the opening of the railway, which caused a decrease of dues from £6,000 in 1846 to less than £1,000 in 1865. (E.H. Gooch, *A History of Spalding*, 1940)

Vessels with Spalding Crews, 1891 Census

Vessel	Crew	Type	Tonnage	Where Registered	Position at Time of Census
John	James Charles Atkin, Capt.	Sloop	47 tons	Registered Lynn	At Methley
	Thomas (Tot) Atkin, Mate				
John and Elizabeth	Thomas Dunn, Capt.	Sailing Coasting	50 tons	Registered Goole	Moored at Hunt's Works
Gelaten	Samuel Grassam, Able Seaman	Schooner	133 tons	Registered Padstow	River Wear, Sunderland
Sarah	Tom Richard Hack	Sailing Coasting	59 tons	Registered Goole	River Wear, Sunderland
	William Warby, Mate				

Nantes	Robert Gosterlow, Capt.	Screw Steamer	179 tons	Registered London	Off Gravesend
	John Royce, Mate				

1891 Census, Spalding

Name	Occupation	Address
Joseph Kitchen	Mariner	Commercial Road
Robert Hayes	Retired Mariner	Commercial Road
Edward Royce	Fisherman	Commercial Road
Joseph Gostelow	Retired Mariner	Commercial Road
John R. Grassam	Master Mariner	Albert Street
William C. Hurrey	Mariner	Willow Row Walk

White's Directory 1892

Name	Occupation	Address
James Atkin	Barge Owner	29 Albert Street
James Charles Atkin	Master Mariner	19a Willow Walk
Robert Arthur Hayes	Barge Owner	43 Albert Street
Edward Royce	Boat Owner and Fisherman	Hope Cottage, Commercial Road
Wade Stedman	Master Mariner	Little London
John Turner	Barge Owner	The Angel, 35 Double Street

8

Shipping Memories of Some Spalding Residents

The following selection of memories of Spalding and the river as they were in the nineteenth and early twentieth centuries have been published before and will be of interest to readers, as they are beyond the memory of most people living today.

The River Welland frozen, around 1892–95. (F. Parkinson, Chain Bridge Forge collection)

River Welland
frozen: a view
looking upstream.
(F. Parkinson, SGS
collection)

I was 18 years old when I went to sea in a sailing vessel. There was a nice
trade done on the River Welland then, but not like there had been. There
was a good trade in coals from the North of England and foreign ships used
to come up with deals to Fosdyke Bridge when there was a heavy draught
of water.

Our boats took cargoes of wheat and flour and carrots in the winter time.
I have taken carrots and apples and different things to the North of England.

My mother once saw 39 vessels in the river and there were 375 came up
in one year. The biggest barge I ever remember coming up was the *Harwich*
of Harwich laden with timber and flax. I was about forty years in the trade,
mostly to Middlesbrough, Sunderland, Seaham, London and on the coasting
trade generally. My boat was the *Sarah* of 40 tons, which would load 70 tons;
we could carry 20 quarters of wheat.

I can remember the chief captains of the old days: Sam Culpin, Gosterlow, Hays, Royce, Chester, Joe Vine, Matthew Vine, and John and Joseph Atkin.

One of our Spalding boats, John Gosterlow's, was lost with all hands on a Christmas Eve making haste to get home from the North. The Captain and three men were on board. (Captain John Turner of Spalding (1839–1926), 'When the Welland was busy', *Spalding Free Press*, 25 November 1919).

Capt. John Knott and three of his sons sailed regularly from Spalding to the northern and southern ports, but one tide they did not turn up as usual, nor the next, or ever, for the ship had gone down with father and three sons.[1] His remaining son gained his certificates as an officer in the mercantile marine. He erected a tombstone to his father and brothers in Spalding cemetery and when visiting his native town, after his mother had died, made his home with his great friend Mr. George Hall, the auctioneer. But he, like his father and brothers, eventually failed to return to port ...[2]

Sailors lived very badly in those days, mainly hard biscuits and salt pork for breakfast, dinner, and supper, and rarely anything else. Mrs. Turner and her first husband, Mr. William Blades, were ship chandlers and supplied most of the vessels that sailed to and from Spalding with the necessities of life, the chief of them being biscuits ...

The old skippers were a generous lot and liberal with their money when in port. Large profits were not only sometimes made on their cargoes, but a great deal of smuggling went on also and some of them were exceedingly clever in evading the custom officers, especially the womenfolk, who often went to sea with their husbands. There was one notorious character named Mrs. Payne who acted as mate on her husband's ship: she would take full charge and let her husband go to bed, but in rough weather she would always take the tiller and steer the vessel herself, and when it rained she always put her umbrella up whilst performing her duties, and if the ship was expected in

---

1 This is not true as the gravestone in Spalding cemetery has the following inscription: 'Thomas Knott, lost at sea off Scarborough, December 20 1837, aged 48 years. Henry Knott lost off Dimlington, January 17 1842, aged 17 years. Thomas Knott, lost in the Bristol Channel, November 24 1852, aged 22 years. John Knott, drowned in the Thames, May 20 1869, aged 46 years.'

2 20 May 1884, *Spalding Free Press*: 'The *Buckinghamshire* of London, that left Shields for Rangoon with coals on October 2 1883, was spoken to in Latitude 21 N, Longitude 40 W, on January 7. [The Chief Mate, William Knott of Spalding] was on last Wednesday posted at Lloyds as missing. We have reason to fear that the ship has been lost with all hands.'

Spalding on a rainy day the boys would be on the look-out to see old mother Payne at the tiller with her famous umbrella …

Captain George Levesley was skipper of Mr. Henry Bugg's yacht. Mr. Bugg was the proprietor of the brewery and a very wealthy man whose chief hobby was the sea …

Mr. Edward Bennett, who died in 1933, age 94, remembered his father and brother, who were carpenters and joiners, fitting up this yacht in a luxurious manner, and he said it was a very expensive hobby. Dar Royce was one of the crew of this yacht when a young man and they went down to the Isle of Wight for a few weeks. Being a sailor, he soon made himself popular with one of the opposite sex there, who persuaded him to marry her, which he agreed to do. The banns were read in church and he eventually led her to the altar, and on the parson saying, 'Will you have this woman to be your wedded wife?' Royce lifted up his head and said, 'Would you, sir?' And on the clergyman answering, 'No, no, my man, certainly not!' he said, 'Well, then, neither will I' and he ran out of church and left her. The inhabitants were exceedingly indignant at his behaviour and threatened to lynch, and when Mr. Bugg heard the reason, they weighed anchor quickly and cleared away from that unhealthy spot …

The Royces were a well-known family of mariners, there being many of that name engaged in our river trade and elsewhere. Tom Royce owned the *Roarer*, which was lost, though he and his crew were saved, but unfortunately it was not insured. He also owned the Laurel and William Royce. Ted Royce had the *Hope*, and Capt. Turner, Tom Royce's stepbrother had the *Sarah* and the *Violet*. Toby and Joe Royce were both, at different times, cut off by the tides whilst duck-shooting on the sands in the Wash, and were drowned. Tom Dunn owned a ship called the *Elizabeth Ann*, and he was notorious for being the most careful skipper from these parts, and if the weather did not look promising he would stay at the mouth of the river until it did. Once he and his crew stayed there for five weeks before venturing out to sea, but they hadn't proceeded far before a storm suddenly burst upon them, which made them take to their boats and quickly row to the Lincolnshire coast. They thought their abandoned ship had been lost, and on arriving in Spalding they proceeded to spend some of the money which was anticipated from her insurance, but they soon heard it had been salved by some Lynn men and taken into port and they were going to sue him for salvage to the amount of 40 per cent of the total value. Poor Tommy Dunn, the fates were against him …

There were many notorious mariners of the Culpin family, and Richard Culpin followed Richard Culpin one generation after another. The Culpins traded chiefly in pots and hardware, building a warehouse in Double Street to store what their ships brought from Hull, Newcastle etc. Mrs. Culpin often went to sea and was very clever at hiding tobacco, etc. from prying eyes of the custom officers by concealing dutiable goods under her crinoline skirt. They did a prosperous trade and retired very well off, owning a good deal of property in the town …

Mrs. Turner's brother, Edwin Goute, was captain of his own ship and traded with the Baltic ports. Once during a bad storm, his chief mate was washed overboard, and his crew of foreigners got panicky and refused to obey orders, they proceeded to lower the boats from their davits and he had to go among them and threaten to shoot with his pistols unless they obeyed orders and resumed their duties. The barrels had broken loose and were smashing about the deck, before they could be secured, one dashed into him and bashed his leg to pulp, he was in terrible agony for days until they at last arrived in England, when he had his leg off, but otherwise he recovered and went to sea again …

Another fine old family was the Atkins, who for many generations followed the sea.

One son was lost from his vessel in Hamburg, or at least he went ashore there and was never heard of again …

Capt. Bob Atkin was tried for murder in London. He had taken a cargo, in his own ship, to London and whilst lying in the river was boarded by some river thieves and he, in naturally defending his property against the invaders, killed one of them. Of course he was arrested and spent the usual lengthy time awaiting trial. He was eventually acquitted …

Another Spalding skipper, Capt. Walker, had his ship quarantined off Gravesend when taking cargo to London, because one of his crew had smallpox. He also contracted the malady and died onboard …

Once, during a very severe winter, fourteen ships were frozen up in the ice between Spalding and Cowhirne and had to remain there for several weeks …

Mrs. Crookes, the wife of Capt. Crookes, went down the river in a small boat with some friends to meet her husband's ship which was due, but the boat was caught in an exceptionally big eagre,[1] near the mouth of the river, which threw Mrs. Crookes out and she was drowned …

Captain Joe Gosterlow was a popular skipper of these parts, the last of his line as a mariner trading from Spalding. He owned a ship called the *Mary*

---

1 The 'eagre' was a wave caused by the rising tide entering the narrow embanked river, much like the Trent Aegir. I remember it coming up as far as the Albert (Chain) Bridge when I was a boy.

Jane and was bringing a cargo of coals from Newcastle to the gasworks at Spalding early in 1895, but he never arrived, for the vessel went down with all hands off the Humber. His crew of three was all local lads, Simon Marsh, Lineham, and Willcox, and the tragedy cast a gloom over the district, for they were all popular among a wide circle of friends. (Extracts from 'Tales of the Sea', an interview with Mrs Turner that appears in E.H. Gooch, *A History of Spalding*, 1940)

Mrs Smalley of Albion Street, Spalding, was the daughter of Mr and Mrs Ellis Pannell of the shipyard, Marsh Road, Spalding. Pannell's boatbuilding yard was started when a slip was laid down in the River Welland bank in 1837 by John Pannell, who had started the family boatbuilding and carpentry business at the Jolly Crispin Inn near Chain Bridge in 1822. John died in 1843 and was succeeded by his son Ellis Pannell. Mrs Smalley lived for a good deal of her life by the side of the River Welland and told of the flourishing old river trade.

She remembered the days when the bigger vessels turned round opposite the Vine Inn. The biggest ship she remembered was the schooner *W.S. Howard*, and she also recalled other schooners, lighters, sailing vessels and billy-boys that plied to and fro.

She also stated that there were several large cranes along by the river and large boats came right up to High Bridge. Numerous vessels unloaded

The Aegir, in a postcard postmarked 22 December 1915.

near where Messrs Grooms' wood yard was on High Street. She recalled one exceptionally large crane on the river bank opposite The Limes in Double Street.

Mrs Smalley said that Herring Lane became so named because of the large number of fish that were sold along there, and that there were towing paths on each side of the river all the way to Fosdyke and horses could pull lighters and barges right down to the sea.

She was married in 1870 and recalls that on the morning of the wedding there were nineteen vessels moored in the river between their house and High Bridge and to celebrate the event her father was called to supply half a gallon of ale to each vessel.

The town in those days, she said, was full of inns and public houses, especially along by the river where nearly every house was inhabited by a ship's captain or a member of the crew of a ship. A former occupant of her own house was a Captain Stanley Jackson, who was buried in the garden. The stone slab that bore the date of death, 1842, and an inscription was still in the garden, although reversed. (Mrs Smalley's recollections were published in the *Lincolnshire, Boston & Spalding Free Press*, 30 September 1940, p. 2.)

A drawing by Edward Gentle showing the river in the mid-1800s, busy with vessels. (Postcard, *Lincolnshire Free Press*)

Vessels in the river viewed from Albion Street, by Edward Gentle. (Postcard, *Lincolnshire Free Press*)

Mr J.E. Pannell, of Marsh Road, Spalding, who came of an old shipbuilding family, could remember when the Welland at Spalding was packed with schooners and billy-boys to the High Bridge:

About a hundred years ago his grandfather, Mr John Pannell, founded a ship building and carpentering business on the banks of the Welland along the Marsh Road, near the old slipway sloping towards the river, which is all that remains, apart from warehouses and granaries, to remind us that Spalding was once a port of considerable importance. Mr Pannell, who is apparently the last owner of the business, succeeded to it in 1888, when it was not unusual for the Welland to be frozen over for several weeks with the result that boats could not get away. When the ice thawed quite a fleet of them would go out on the same tide. The cargoes were chiefly coal, wood, cake or maize etc. Timber sometimes came from as far afield as the Baltic and good a number of men got a living as riverside porters.

Mr Pannell recalled the names of some of the boats in quick succession. There were *Sarah*, *Breeze*, *Mary Jane*, *Samuel*, *George*, *Active*, *Bounty*, *Elizabeth*, *Aurora*, *Mary*, *Catherine*, *William and George*, *John* and others of from fifty to

Pannell's boatyard on Marsh Road. (F. Parkinson, Spalding Gentlemen's Society collection)

A view from the boatyard looking downstream towards Pigeon End. (F. Parkinson, Spalding Gentlemen's Society collection)

one hundred and twenty tons, all belonging to the local traders and mariners. The boats did their best to reach home for Christmas. Mr Pannell remembers the building of various boats, including Mr Henry Bugg's yacht *Red Rover*, which was launched sideways into the river over sixty years ago. Mr George Levesley, of Spalding, was her captain. (Extracts from E.H.Gooch, *A History of Spalding*, 1940)

9

SHIPPING NEWS FROM LOCAL NEWSPAPERS

The newspapers local to the River Welland had shipping news after the 'births, marriages and deaths' column in the weeks when there were sailings in or out of port. Sometimes there would be several weeks when no vessels were able to come in or leave because of bad weather or a lack of water in the river due to low tides.

Lincoln, Rutland & Stamford Mercury

22 NOVEMBER 1813
The vessel *The Juliet* of Spalding sank in the Humber.

Spalding Shipping News from Drakard's *Stamford News*

The first is the vessel's name followed by the captain's name:

10 JULY 1818
Arrived *Welcome Messenger* Dudding with bricks and tiles; *Neptune* Mason with cobbles; *Samuel and William* Lowery with goods, all from Hull. *Three Sisters* Knott with cobbles from Blackney and Cley. *Union* Turpin with groceries etc. from London.
Sailed *Union* Turpin; *Three Sisters* Knott both for London with oats.

16 OCTOBER 1818
Arrived *Alpha* Wilcox from Sunderland with coals and glass bottles. *John* Acaster, *Rambler* Cambell both from Hull with timber. *Trial* Burkenshaw

from London with goods. *Welcome Messenger* Dudding with bricks and tiles; *John and Mary Ann* Haley with Baltic goods, both from Hull. *Betsy* Freeman from Lynn with timber.

4 SEPTEMBER 1819

Arrived *Wellington* Johnson with linseed cakes; *Three Brothers* Canby with Baltic goods, both from Hull, and *Industry* Royce from London with groceries.

18 SEPTEMBER 1819

Arrived *Hannah* Broughton, *Ebenezer* Rhodes, *William and Ellen* Medgem, all from Hull with coals and linseed cakes. *Neptune* Mason, *Nancy* White, both from London with goods.

Sailed *Neptune* Mason, *Hannah* Broughton both for Hull with wool. *Ann and Elizabeth* Booth for Lynn; *Nancy* White for London, both with oats.

Stamford Herald & County Chronicle

TO 10 NOVEMBER 1830

Arrived *Providence* Copley from Goole with coals. *Jane* Smith from London with goods.

Sailed *Blessing* Turner for Yarmouth with oats. *Two Marys* Thompson for Selby and *Industry* Booth for Goole, both with wheat.

17 NOVEMBER 1830

Arrived *Ceto* Pakey from Selby; *Fly* Ward & *Triton* Knight from Goole, all coal laden. *Wellington* White with groceries etc. from London.

3 DECEMBER 1830

Arrived *Mayflower* Gregory, *Industry* Booth, *Ann & Elizabeth* Gosterlow & *Unity* Rear from Goole; *Sovereign* Barker from Stockton & *Thomas & Ann* Bartrup from Selby, all with coal. *Dove* Lowery Snr & *Martha* Lowery jnr from Hull with goods, deals etc.

Sailed *Bee* Royce, *Thomas & Jane* Seymour, *Triton* Knight, *Albion* Ward, *John & Maria* Jackson & *Good Intent* Barton for Selby, all with wheat. *Industry* Wright for Goole with potatoes. *Wellington* White with oats & *Jane* Smith with flour & oats, both for London.

8 DECEMBER 1830
Arrived None
Sailed *Good Intent* Barton, *Ann & Elizabeth* Gosterlow, *Industry* Booth, *Ceto* Pakey & *Thomas & Ann* Bartrup for Selby & *Ann & Elizabeth* Seymour for Goole, all with wheat & beans. *Dove* Lowery for Hull with potatoes.

15 DECEMBER 1830
Arrived *Nautilus* Brighton, *Fly* Ward & *Mantura* Mimmack from Sunderland & *Welland* Rogers from Goole, all with corn.
Sailed *Endeavours Increase* Wilkinson for Hull with potatoes.

22 DECEMBER 1830
Arrived *Two Marys* Thompson from Goole; *Endeavor* Turner from Selby, both with coals. *Glen* Draper from London & *Charlotte* Cook from Hull both with goods.
Sailed *Welland* Rogerson, *Two Marys* Thompson & *Fly* Ward for Goole & *Thomas & Elizabeth* Green for Selby, all with wheat.

12 JANUARY 1831
Arrived *Good Intent* Barton, *Thomas & Ann* Seymour and *Blessing* Turner from Goole, all with coal. *Bee* Royce with linseed and *Albion* Wilkinson with tiles from Hull.

12 JANUARY 1831
Sailed *Fly* Ward and *Mantura* Mimmack for Selby with wheat. *Glen* Draper for London with oats and flour.

19 JANUARY 1831
Arrived *Oak* Mawer and *Ceto* Pakey from Selby; *Industry* Wright, *Ann & Elizabeth* J. Gosterlow, *Joseph & Ann* W. Gosterlow and *Thomas & Ann* Bartrup from Goole, all coal laden. *William* Butler and *Hope* Cole from Boston with slates. *Bee* Lowery jnr with goods and *Dove* Lowery Snr. with linseed cakes from Hull. *Wellington* White from London with goods.
Sailed *Charlotte and Eliza* Culpin, *Two Brothers* Jackson and *Mayflower* Gregory for Selby; *Ancholm* Chapman, *Nautilus* Brighton, *Bee* Royce, *Blessing* Turner, *Thomas & Jane* Seymour and *Oak* Mawer for Goole; *Jason* Snowden for London, all laden with corn and flour.

26 JANUARY 1831

Arrived *Three Brothers* Hargrave from Hull with coal.

Sailed *Ceto* Pakey and *John & Joseph* Gosterlow for Goole; *Thomas & Ann* Bartrup for Selby; *Dove* Lowery for Hull and *Good Intent* Barton for London, all with corn.

2 FEBRUARY 1831

Arrived *Robert & William* Lister and *Three Brothers* Hargrave and *Metcalf* Jarvis for London; *Thomas & Ann* Bartrup for Selby; *Industry* Wright and *Jane* Smith for Goole, all with corn.

16 FEBRUARY 1831

Arrived *Elizabeth* Seymour, *Thomas & Ann* Green, *Industry* Chalner, *Charlotte & Elizabeth* Culpin and *Daisy* Kirk from Goole and *Industry* Booth from Selby, with coals. *Providence* Marshall from Boston with slates. *Fanny* Wrigglesworth with linseed cakes and timber, and *Martha* Lowery with goods, both from Hull. *Glen* Draper from London with goods.

Sailed *Bee* Townend, *Robert & William* Lister and *Elizabeth* Seymour for Goole with wheat, beans & oats. *Three Brothers* Hargrave for London with oats.

23 FEBRUARY 1831

Arrived *Two Marys* Thompson and *Fly* Ward from Goole with coals. *Two Brothers* Jackson from Hull with deals.

Sailed *Triton* Knight and *Thomas & Elizabeth* Green for Goole; *Industry* Booth for Hull; *Kitty* Shepherd and *Fanny* Wrigglesworth for London, with corn and flour.

2 MARCH 1831

Arrived *Welland* Rogerson from Goole with coals. *Charlotte* Cook from Hull with linseed cakes, timber and deals.

Sailed *Martha* Lowry and *Two Marys* Thompson for Goole with beans and oats. *Glen* Draper and *Daisy* Kirk for London with oats and malt.

16 MARCH 1831

Arrived *Friendship* J. Royce and *Bee* P. Royce, *Mayflower* Gregory and *Endeavour* Turner from Goole; *Wentworth* Rhodes and *Alert* Wake from Selby, all with coals. *Wellington* White from London and *Providence* Copley from Hull, with groceries etc.

Sailed *Ancholm* Chapman and *Three Brothers* Teed for London; *Fly* Ward and *Thomas & Jane* Seymour for Goole; *Industry* Booth for Hull, all with corn.

23 MARCH 1831
Arrived *Brothers* England, *Ann & Elizabeth* J. Gosterlow, *Elizabeth* Seymour, *Joseph & Ann* W. Gosterlow and *Jane* Smith from Goole; *Industry* Wright from Selby, all with coal. *Good Intent* Barton from London with goods.
Sailed *Blessing* Turner, *Bee* Royce, *Albion* Wilkinson, *Ceto* Pakey and *Wentworth* Marshall for Goole with corn. *Mayflower* Gregory with potatoes and *Industry* Booth with corn, both for Hull.

30 MARCH 1831
Arrived *Martha* Lowery and *Endeavour* Cawthorne from Hull with deals, timber and linseed cakes. *Charlotte & Eliza* Culpin from Goole with sundries.
Sailed *Industry* Booth with beans and *Providence* Copley with potatoes, both for Hull. *Wellington* White, *Harbinger* Ward, *Jane* Smith and *Good Intent* Barton for London with oats, beans and flour.

6 APRIL 1831
Arrived *Thomas & Elizabeth* Green from Selby with coals.

APRIL 6 1831
Sailed *Ann & Elizabeth* Gosterlow for Selby with wheat.

13 APRIL 1831
Arrived *Glen* Draper from London and *Dove* Lowery from Hull, both with goods.
Sailed *Spring* Wadingham and *Charlotte & Eliza* Culpin for Goole; *Alert* Wake and *Joseph & Ann* Gosterlow both for London, with corn and flour.

20 APRIL 1831
Arrived *Martha* Lowery and *Mayflower* Gregory from Hull with deals and goods. *William & Jane* Henesley from Selby with coals.
Sailed *Brothers* England for Goole with beans. *Glen* Draper for London with oats and flour.

27 APRIL 1831

Arrived *William & Jane* Henesley and *Industry* Booth from Selby, both with coals.

Sailed *Two Brothers* Jackson for London with oats.

19 MAY 1831

Arrived *Welland* Rogerson and *Good Intent* Barton from London; *Elizabeth* Stedman and *Bee* Townend from Hull, all with goods. *Friendship* Royce and *Spring* Wadingham from Goole; *Brothers* England and *Barbara* Marshall from Stockton; *Ann* Mountain from Newcastle, with coals.

19 MARCH 1831

Sailed *Wellington* White, *Good Intent* Barton, *Welland* Rogerson, *Thomas & Ann* Bartrup and *George* Wells for London with oats, flour and machinery. *Bee* Royce for Goole with wheat. *Charlotte & Eliza* Culpin and *Ann & Elizabeth* Gosterlow for Selby with wheat and beans.

1 JUNE 1831

Arrived *Metcalf* Jarvis and *Mary Ann* Rowbottom from Goole with coals. *Glen* Draper from London with goods. *Dove* Lowery from Hull with goods and deals.

Sailed *Thomas & Jane* Seymour and *Dove* Lowery for Goole; *Industry* Booth for Selby; *Glen* Draper and *Jane* Smith for London, all with corn.

15 JUNE 1831

Arrived *Two Brothers* Jackson with tiles and *Bee* Townend with goods and deals, both from Hull. *William & Jane* Kinnersley from Selby; *Amicus* Holmes and *Sarah* Thorley from Goole; *Three Sisters* Lund from Sunderland; *Nautilus* Brighton and *Barbara* Marshall from Stockton with corn. *Wellington* White from London with goods.

Sailed *Industry* Wright and *Ann* Ward for London; *Argossy* Broughton for Goole; *Ann & Elizabeth* Gosterlow and *Charlotte & Eliza* Gosterlow for Selby, all with corn.

29 JUNE 1831

Arrived *Endeavour* Turner, *Eagle* Bateman, *Joseph & Ann* Gosterlow, *Luna* Moore, *Sarah* Thorley, *Brothers* England and *Bee* Royce from Goole; *Industry* Booth from Selby; *Betsy* Carmikle, *Two Marys* Thompson, *Fly* Ward and *Two Brothers* Jackson from Sunderland; *Rose* Howell, *Sarah* Martinson and

Three Brothers Pearson from Stockton; *Friendship* Royce and *Blessing* Turner from Newcastle, with coals. *Dove* Lowery from Hull with goods, timber and deals.

Sailed *Thomas & Ann* Bartrup for Selby with wheat and beans. *Industry* Booth for Hull with beans.

13 JULY 1831

Arrived *Daisy* Elleries, *Three Brothers* Hargrave, *Argossy* Broughton, *Friendship* Royce, *Metcalf* Jarvis, *Three Johns* Rhodes and *Amicus* Holmes with coals; *Joseph & Ann* Gosterlow with goods, all from Goole. *Two Brothers* Jackson from Sunderland with goods.

Sailed *Ceto* Pakey for Goole; *Good Intent* Barton and *Welland* Rogerson for London, all with corn.

27 JULY 1831

Arrived *Martha* Lowery, *Mary & Elizabeth* Coats and *Joseph & Ann* Gosterlow from Sunderland; *Endeavour* Cawthorne, *Ann* Ward and *Blessing* Turner from Newcastle; *Industry* Booth from Goole, all with coal. *Emperor* Clark from Selby and *Albion* Wilkinson from London, both with goods.

Sailed *Bee* P. Royce and *Ann & Elizabeth* Gosterlow for Goole with wheat and beans. *Friendship* J. Royce with oats and *Jane* Smith with freestone, both for London. *Bee* Townend for Hull with goods.

10 AUGUST 1831

Arrived *Iris* Burkinshaw and *Wentworth* Marshall from Sunderland; *Argossy* Broughton, *Ceto* Pakey, *Brothers* England and *Bee* Royce from Goole, all with coal. *Wellington* White and *Good Intent* Barton from London and *Dove* Lowery from Hull, with goods.

Sailed *Glen* Draper for London with flour, oats and stone. *Industry* Booth for Goole with beans.

25 AUGUST 1831

Arrived *Sarah* Martinson, *Ann* Y. Ward and *Fly* B. Ward from Sunderland; *Joseph & Ann* Gosterlow, *Robert & William* Lister and *Industry* Wright from Goole, all with coals. *Bee* Townend and *Dove* Lowery from Hull with deals etc.

31 AUGUST 1831

Arrived *Charlotte & Eliza* Culpin, *Wentworth* Marshall, *William & Jane* Kinnersley and *Bee* Royce from Goole, all with coals. *Jane* Smith and *Welland* Rogerson from London with goods.

Sailed *Charlotte & Eliza* Culpin for Goole with wheat and beans.

14 SEPTEMBER 1831

Arrived *Grimsthorpe Castle* Haw, *Albion* Wilkinson, *Friendship* Royce and *Susannah* Hill from Goole, all with coals. *Glen* Draper from London with groceries etc.

Sailed *Grimsthorpe Castle* Haw, *Industry* Wright, *Emperor* and *Bee* Royce for Goole with wheat, beans and rapeseed.

5 OCTOBER 1831

Arrived *Ceto* Pakey from Lynn; *Ann* Y.Ward from Newcastle; *Two Brothers* Jackson, *Fly* B.Ward and *Jane* Smith from Goole, all with coals.

Sailed *Patrick* Finney and *Unity* Brakes for Goole with wheat and wool. *Fly* B.Ward for London with oats, wheat and flour.

12 OCTOBER 1831

Arrived *Two Brothers* Jackson, *Friendship* Royce, *Lamb* Draper, *Charlotte & Eliza* Bear, *Oak & Standard* Goodyear, *Grimsthorpe Castle* Haw, *John Pearson* Johnson, *Two Marys* Thompson, *Charlotte* Dudding, *Ceto* Pakey, *Jane* Smith and *Ann* Marshall from Goole, all with coals. *Good Intent* Barton from London with goods.

Sailed *Ann* Ward for London with oats and freestone.

26 OCTOBER 1831

Arrived *Bee* Royce, *Industry* Wright, *Martin* Thompson, *Three Brothers* Pearson, *Emperor* Clark, *Industry* Booth, *Argossy* Broughton, *Ann & Elizabeth* Gosterlow, *Sarah* Mariimson and *Susanah* Hill from Goole; *Daisy* Elwes and *Ann & Elizabeth* Coats from Stockton and *Joseph & Ann* Gosterlow from Selby, all coal laden. *Dove* Lowry, *Bee* Townend, *Betsy* Willcox and *Success* Hossell with goods, deals and linseed cakes, all from Hull.

26 OCTOBER 1831

Sailed *Glen* Draper and *Jane* Smith with flour, wheat and oats for London. *Charlotte & Eliza* Bear and *Elizabeth* Steadman with wheat for Lynn. *Industry*

Booth, *Thomas & Jane* Seymour and *Industry* Wright with wheat and beans for Goole.

2 NOVEMBER 1831

Arrived *Albion* Wilkinson, *Two Brothers* Jackson, *Unity* Brakes, *Thomas & Ann* Bartrupt, *Two Marys* Thompson, *Thomas & Elizabeth* Green and *Lamb* Draper from Goole; *Sisters* Barker from Stockton, all coal laden.
Sailed None.

9 NOVEMBER 1831

Arrived *Robert & Frances* Richmond and *Daisy* Elwes from Newcastle; *Elizabeth* Steadman from Lynn; *Three Brothers* Pearson, *Friendship* Royce, *Mayflower* Gregory, *Ann & Elizabeth* Gosterlow, *Patriot* Finny, *Wentworth* Marshall, *Fame* Hargrave and *Metcalf* Jarvis from Goole, all coal laden.
Sailed *Argossy* Broughton for Goole with wheat. *John Pearson* Johnson and *Good Intent* Barton for London with wheat, oats and flour.

23 NOVEMBER 1831

Arrived *Charlotte & Eliza* Bear, *Marten* Thompson, *Joseph & Ann* Gosterlow, *Industry* Booth, *Industry* Wright, *Thomas & Jane* Seymour, *Merchantman* Watson, *Wentworth* Marshall, *Two Marys* Thompson, *Mary & Elizabeth* Coates, *Two Brothers* Jackson, *Thomas & Elizabeth* Green from Goole and *Robert & Frances* from Newcastle, all coal laden.
Sailed *Albion* Wilkinson, *Lark* Marriot and *Charlotte & Eliza* Bear for Lynn, all with wheat. *Welland* Rogerson, *Lamb* Draper, *Three Brothers* Pearson and *Mary Ann* Culpin for London, all with wheat, flour and freestone.

30 NOVEMBER 1831

Arrived *Metcalf* Jarvis and *Freedom* Tomlinson from Goole with coals. *Glen* Draper from London with goods.
Sailed *Wentworth* Marshall, *Thomas & Elizabeth* Green and *Thomas & Jane* Seymour all for London with wheat, flour and oats. *Industry* Wright for Goole with wheat.

14 DECEMBER 1831

Arrived *Elizabeth* Turner, *Two Brothers* Jackson and *Ann* Ward, all with coals from Goole. *Good Intent* Barton with goods from London.
Sailed *Bee* Royce with wheat for Goole.

22 DECEMBER 1831

Arrived *Argossy* Broughton and *Ann* Ward both from Goole with coals. *Betsy* Willcox from Hull with deals and coals. *Jane* Smith from London with groceries.

Sailed *Friendship* Royce, *Mary & Elizabeth* Coats and *Dove* Lowey for Goole; *Elizabeth & Ann* Turner and *Jane* Smith for London, all laden with grain & flour.

28 DECEMBER 1831

Arrived *Ann & Elizabeth* J. Gosterlow, *Lamb* Draper, *Albion* Wilkinson, *Joseph & Ann* W. Gosterlow and *Susannah* Hill from Goole with coals. *Martha* Lowey and *Bee* Townend from Hull; *Welland* Rogerson from London, all with goods.

Sailed *Mary Ann* Culpin, *Argossy* Broughton, *Lamb* Draper, *Ann & Elizabeth* Gosterlow, *Elizabeth* Steadman and *Ceto* Pakey for Goole; *Good Intent* Barton and *Three Brothers* Pearson for London, all laden with grain & flour.

Extract from *Lincolnshire in 1836*

The number of vessels and amount of tonnage outwards and inwards during the years 1829 to 1836 both inclusive.

Year	Vessels in	Vessels out	Tonnage in	Tonnage out
1829	250	143	12,523	7,138
1830	293	176	14,431	8,676
1831	325	187	16,044	9,059
1832	452	209	22,062	10,286
1833	462	282	22,712	13,951
1834	411	226	20,718	11,398
1835	465	232	23,387	10,928

Lincoln, Rutland & Stamford Mercury

TO 19 FEBRUARY 1840

Arrived *Mary* Jewitt & *Industry* Bear from Goole with coals. *Reform* Goodson from Hull with deals, timber & goods.

Sailed *Lark* Carter for Blakney & *William* Althrope for Lynn, both with oak timber. *Industry* Robinson with wheat and *Trial* Day with ale & carrots, both for Newcastle. *Ancholm* Hill, *Emperor* Clark & *Tryphena* Proctor for Goole with wheat & beans & *Adventurer* Rylatt for London with oats.

TO 26 AUGUST 1840

Arrived *Two Brothers* Green from Newcastle; *Joseph & Ann* White from Goole; *William & J Marsden* Carmichael from Stockton, all coal laden. *New Good Intent* Burton from London with goods.

TO 17 FEBRUARY 1841

Arrived *Alert* Hall from Goole with coals. *Glen* Draper from London.

TO 28 JULY 1841

Arrived *Sarah* Jackson, *Jane* Payne & *Stamford* Townend from Hull; *Mary* Jewitt, *Glen* Draper, *Faith* Jewitt & *Tryphena* Proctor from Stockton & *Ann & Jane* Swan, *Jane* Cheffings & *Welland* Johnson from Goole, all with coals, goods etc.
Sailed *Bee* Hayes, *Freedom* Royce, *Elizabeth* Jackson & *Emperor* Clark for Goole & *John & Ann* Seymou; & *Lamb* White for Newcastle, all with grain.

TO 1 DECEMBER 1841

Arrived *Betsy* Levesley, *Mary Ann* Rodwell & *Bee* Hayes from Goole; *Meadburn* Pattison & *Echo* Tupman from Newcastle; *Freedom* Royce from London & *Sally* Booth from Lynn, all with cake, goods etc.
Sailed *Merchantman* Watson & *Diligent* Payne for London; *Sisters* Walker, *Rose* Crosskill, *Sarah* Cottom, *John* Welldrake, *Margaret* Audlin, *John & Mary* Smith & *Three Sisters* Raddings for Goole, all with grain & fruit.

TO 9 APRIL 1843

Arrived *Charlotte* Tulley from Hull; *Ancholm* Vine, *Friends* Levesley, *Mary* Greenhall, *John & Hannah's Endeavour* Servent, *John Pearson* Duckering, *Nine Brothers* Pybus, *Mary Ann* Culpin, *Tryphena* Proctor, *Elizabeth* Thompson, *Lamb* Wilkinson, *George* Simpson from Goole; *John* Stell, from Selby; *May* Chester from Stockton & *Freedom* Royce & *Diligent* Payne from London with goods, stone etc.

TO 19 APRIL 1843

Sailed *Sarah* Jackson for Maldon; *Joseph & Ann* White, *Tryphena* Proctor, *Vigilante* Upton, *May* Chalmer, *Freedom* Royce, *Glen* Draper, *Ann* Taylor, *M. & S. Marsden* Crooks, *Martha* Greenhall for London; *Diligent* Payne for Leith; *Martha* Townend for Hull; *William* Levesley for Lynn; *New Good Intent* Upton for Newcastle & *John* Still, *Ancholm* Vine, *George* Shipman, *Ann* Johnson; *Lamb* Wilkinson & *Lark* Chester for Goole, all with wheat, grain etc.

TO 13 DECEMBER 1843

Arrived *Thomas & Martha* Hutton & *Sea* Wilkinson from Stockton; *Martha* Cliff from Hartlepool; *Mary* Greenhall from Newcastle; *Pommane* Hender, *Sussana* Palmer, *Active* Owen & *Elizabeth* Jackson from Hull; *Jane* Etty, *Henry & Ann* Woodhead, *Charity* Cawthorne, *Ancholm* Vine & *Billow* Walker from Goole; *William* Levesley from Lynn; *Urania* Draper, *Laurel* Green & *Industry* Wright from London, all with goods, coal, deals, cake etc.

Sailed *Joseph & Elizabeth* Eyre, *Metcalf* Dunn & *Urania* Draper, *Echo* Tupman, *Industry* Beltham & *C.P.T.* Bennett for London; *John & Ann* Seymour for Maldon *John & Jane* Bingham & *William* Levesley for Lynn; *Lamb* Wilkinson, *Easter* Williams, *York* Nicholls, *Tryphena* Proctor, *Martha* Adwick & *Sisters* Draper for Goole & *Wave* Manning & *Wellington* White; for Stockton, all with grain, wheat, potatoes, etc.

Corn shipped during the week wheat 4,500 quarters, grain 800 quarters, flour 50 sacks.

TO 22 DECEMBER 1847

Arrived *Glen* Draper from Dunkirk with oilcake. *Henry & Ann* Simpson, *Three Johns* Cookson, *W.S.R.* Wetherall & *Mary & S Marsden* from Goole; *Princess Royal* Siddal from Ipswich & *John & Jane* Woodhead from Lynn, all with coals, railway chairs, grain etc.

Sailed *John & Jane* Woodhead for Lynn; *Exeter* Jewitt, *Henry & Ann* Simpson, *Sea* Collins, *George & Susanah* Storr for Goole & *Elizabeth* Jackson for Hull, all with grain flour etc.

31 DECEMBER 1847

On Friday morning last about 6 o'clock a fine schooner, *Catherine*, Capt. Shand, Master, from Newport with 100 tons of railway line, for Spalding, was coming up the brushwork near Fosdyke bridge whilst the tide was receding. She rolled over, and is likely to be lost. The cargo is estimated to be at £3,000.

7 JANUARY 1848

A contract has been taken by Messers John & Robert Richardson, ship builders of Boston & Spalding to raise the schooner *Catherine*, which vessel lies in a dangerous situation in the river Welland. Little progress has been made during the week in getting the rails out, owing to the vessel being on her broadside, and immersed in water from the starboard side to the main hatchway. About a third of her cargo has been unloaded.

Spalding Ship News in the *Spalding Free Press*

TO 28 FEBRUARY 1848

Arrived *Margaret* Jackson, *Laurel* Green, *Isabella* Acaster, *John & Ann* Seymour; *Ellen* Crooks, *Sisters* Belsham, *Wellington* Atkin, *Accommodation* Taylor, *Jane* Payne, *Retrenchment* Jackson, *Hope* Taylor and *Thomas and Ann* Colley from Goole; *York* Nichols from Selby; *Perseverance* Hare, *Ellen Jane* Beavis from Newport; *Billow* Walker, *Mary & Elizabeth* Martin and *Ceres* Wright from Ipswich; *Sarah* Jackson from London, with railway iron,[1] chairs, cement, coals, goods etc.

Sailed *William* Watts; *Oak* Redman, *Easter* Jewitt to London; *John & Jane* Woodward to Lynn; *George & Susannah* Storr to Goole, with grain and potatoes.

TO 3 MAY 1848

Arrived *Das Zubruen* Spreckelham from Hamburg with bones.[2] *Thomas and Elizabeth* Storr from Goole; *Ann* Williams from Selby; *John* Cook and *Sussana* Colley from Stockton; *Wellington* Hubbard from Sunderland, with coals, goods etc.

Sailed *Ellen* Vine & *Providence* Taylor to Sunderland with Oak timber etc.

---

1   It is ironic that this shipment of railway iron came by sea, as the arrival of the railway to the town was to take so much trade away from the shipping based on the river.

2   Bones had been imported post-1815, both human and non-human, from the battlefields of Europe: 'The neighborhood of Leipsig, Austerlitz, Waterloo, and of all the places where the principal battles were fought have been swept alike of the bones of the hero and the horse which he rode and thence forwarded to the bone grinders for the purpose of reducing them to a granulated state. In this condition they are sold to the farmer to manure their lands' (from an account published in *The Observer*, 18 November 1822). Hunt and Jennings were listed in a directory as artificial manure manufacturers and bone crushers, Holbeach Road, Steam Bone Mills.

Ancholm Greenhall to Goole; *Enterprise* Rider to Hull; *Urania* Bramhill and *Greenest* Smith to the North; *Happy Jack* Huddlestone to Goole with grain etc.

TO 21 APRIL 1851

Arrived *Hoffnung* Marquard from Hamburg with bones. *Sarah* Jackson & *Ancholm* Greenhall from Stockton; *Susan* Colley from Selby; *Providence* Taylor *Mary* Greenhall and *Happy Jack* Mann from Goole; *Thomas and Ann* Greenhall from Skegness, with coals, grain etc. *Ellen* Vine from London with goods.

Sailed *Ocean* Gosterlow and *Jane* Colley to Goole; *4 Brothers & 4 Sisters* Smith, *Wellington* Hubbard and *Providence* Taylor to Sunderland; *Elizabeth* Jackson to Newcastle with grain, oak timber etc.

TO 5 MAY 1851

Arrived *Wellington* Hubbard from Sunderland and *Emily and Ann* Thompson from Selby with coals; *Haabet* Ishoy from Odesse with barley.

Sailed *Ancholm* Greenhall to Goole; *Enterprise* Rider to Hull; *Ellen* Vine, *Mary & S. Marsden* Knott and *Ocean* Gosterlow to Sunderland; *Sussana* Colley and *Melita* Hays to Newcastle with Grain Oak timber etc. *Emanuel* Wilters, *Das Zubruen* Spreckelham, *Sisters* Ellis, *Mary* Greenhall, *Emily and Ann* Thompson, *John* Cook, *Ann* Williams, *John and Ann* Royce, *Urania* Bramhill, *Happy Jack* Huddlestone, ballast to the North & Humber.

TO 20 JUNE 1851

Arrived *Vrf Gedroeders* Holcher from St Petersberg with oats; *Joseph & Ann* Culpin, *John & Ann* Royce, *Thomas & Jane* Vine & *John* Cook from Middlesborough; *Urania* Bramhill from Hartlepool; *Ancholm* Greenhall from Keadby with coals. *Enterprise* Rider from Hull with general cargo.

Sailed *Melita* Hays to Newcastle; *W.S.R* Crooks to Plymouth with Oak timber, grain etc.

TO 17 JANUARY 1853

Arrived *Providence* Taylor, *Metcalf* Pidd, *Laurel* Green & *Wellington* Green from Hull; *Urania* Pakey, *M. & S. Marsden* Knott, *Lucy Ellen* Neal from Newcastle with coals.

Sailed *David & Ann* Rogers, *Providence* Taylor to Goole with grain.

TO 14 MARCH 1853

Arrived *Laurel* Green from Goole; *Enterprise* Rider from Hull; *Lincoln* Mawer from Stockton, with coals & goods.

Sailed *Ellen* Turner to Goole with grain. *Laurel* Green & *David & Ann* Royce to Goole; *Enterprise* Rider to Hull; *Glen* Wilkinson & *Lincoln* Mawer to the North, in ballast.

14 MARCH 1853

The schooner *John and Ann*, in getting underway at Fosdyke Bridge on Thursday last, during the gale, ran afoul of the sloop *Ellen*, which vessel was safely moored, and forced her on the brushwork, and settling on a pile went through her bottom and filled with water, damaging about 100 quarters of wheat. After stopping the leak in a temporary manner, the vessel was brought up to Spalding to land. The damaged wheat is now being dried.

The loss will be very great to the shipper, a farmer, who resides in the neighborhood and who is not insured. The *Ellen* is now on the stocks being repaired. Great blame is attributed to the master of the *John and Ann* in attempting to move his vessel when the wind was blowing so hard.[1]

TO 9 MAY 1853

Arrived *Joseph & Ann* Culpin from Seaham; *Sarah* Jackson, *John & Ann* Chester from Stockton; *Urania* Gosterlow from Newcastle; *Thomas & Jane*

A sloop like the *Ellen* under repair on the slipway at Pannel's boatyard. (F. Parkinson, Spalding Gentlemen's Society collection)

---

1 Around this time the master of the *Ellen* was my ancestor Captain Vine and the master of the *John and Ann* was a Captain Chester. Later in the same year Captain Vine was master of the *John and Ann*.

A vessel on the slipway. (F. Parkinson, Spalding Gentlemen's Society collection)

Vine & *Wellington* Wade from Sunderland; *Sisters* Ellis from Hartlepool; *Melita* Hays, *Two Sisters* Pakey, *George & Sussana* Storr, *Mary* Greenhall & *Laurel* Green from Goole with coals. *Elizabeth* Jackson & *Enterprise* Rider from Hull with general cargo. *Fos Brid Rapid* Laws from Bremen with bones. **Sailed** *Violet* Dunn to Newcastle with grain. *M. & S. Marsden* Knott, *Hero* Rendall, *Elizabeth* Sharman, *Glen* Wilkinson, *Lucy Ellen* Neal, *Sarah* Jackson, *Joseph & Ann* Culpin, *Melita* Hays to the North in ballast.

TO 26 SEPTEMBER 1853
Arrived *John and Ann* Vine from Middlesborough.

TO 3 DECEMBER 1853
Sailed *John and Ann* Vine to London with oak timber, grain etc.

TO 16 JANUARY 1854

Sailed *W.S.R.* Crooks, *Sea* Greenhall & *Metcalf* Turner to Sunderland with oak timber. *Petrel* Jackson, *Glen* Wilkinson, *Auroa* Richardson, *Urania* Gosterlow, *Susan & Mary* Bruming, *Flora* French, *Friends of Eliza* Hildreth, *Lucy Ellen* Neal, *Greenend* Smith & *Ashton* Coats, all to the North & Humber in ballast.

TO 22 MAY 1854

Arrived *John and Ann* Vine from Ipswich.

TO 5 JUNE 1854

Arrived *John and Ann* Vine from Seaham with coals.

TO 26 JUNE 1854

Sailed *John and Ann* Vine to the North in ballast.

TO 3 JULY 1854

Sailed *Breeze* Levesley to the North in ballast.

TO 10 JULY 1854

Arrived *John and Ann* Vine from Middlesborough.

TO 17 JULY 1854

Arrived *John and Ann* Vine from Goole.

TO 23 OCTOBER 1854

Arrived *Ellen* Vine from Newcastle.

TO 6 NOVEMBER 1854

Arrived *John & Ann* Vine from Sunderland with coals.

TO 1 OCTOBER 1855

Arrived *Wellington* Vine from Goole with coals.

TO 15 OCTOBER 1855

Arrived *Wellington* Vine from Goole with coals.

3 JUNE 1856

The Royal Boston Yacht Club Regatta was held on 30 May. Entries, Mr. Henry Bugg's yacht *Red Rover* 20 tons, skipper Mr. George Levesley,

Mr. Thorpe's *Waterwitch* 15 tons, Mr. Lewin's *Fairy* 17 tons, Mr. Green's *Eugenie* 5 tons, Mr. Marshall's *Kitten* 5 tons, Mr. Anderson's *Magic* 3 tons, Mr. Wilkinson's *Jenny* 7 tons. The course from Maudfoster sluice to Elbow buoy, thence up to Upper-sea-head buoy. During the race the wind got around to the east, still blowing strongly so the capabilities of the yachts were well tested. *Waterwitch* arrived at the mark 1st, *Magic* 2nd, *Fairy* 3rd, and *Kitten* 4th. *Red Rover* got aground and *Jenny* lost her mast.

TO 28 JULY 1856
Sailed *Breeze* Vine to Goole in ballast.[1]

22 SEPTEMBER 1856
Red Rover, the yacht of Mr. Henry Bugg Esq., arrived from Hull.

TO 19 JANUARY 1857
Arrived *Urania* Gosterlow from Newcastle; *Breeze* Vine from Middlesborough; *Laurel* Green, *Hope* Steel, *Violet* Enderby and *Wellington* Atkin from Goole, with coals. *Sea* Greenhall and *Francis* Percy from Hull with coals.
Sailed *Alpha* Aaron with wheat.

Waterwitch, winner of the cup. (Illustrated London News, 14 June 1856)

---

1   This is the earliest reference I have found with Captain Vine as master of the *Breeze*.

TO FEBRUARY 1857

Arrived *Francis* Percy & *Sisters* Ellis from Hull with stone. *Ann* Watson, *Hope* Culpin & *Eagle* Taylor from Goole; *Edwin* Richardson from Middlesborough, with coals. *Ceto* Sutcliff & *Suky* Cowen from Wisbech in ballast.

Sailed *Violet* Enderby to London with wheat. *Ceto* Sutcliff & *Suky* Cowen to Wisbech with potatoes. *Ann* Watson, *Francis* Perry & *Ant* Aisthorpe to the North & Humber in ballast.

TO 2 MARCH 1857

Sailed *Urania* Gosterlow to Penzance with wheat.

TO 25 MAY 1857

Arrived *Margaret* Noble from Gothenburg with deals. *Genius* Heiurick, from Uckermeinde with barley.

Sailed *Red Rover* Henry Bugg Esq. to London; *Mary Ann* Martin to Sunderland, with oak timber.

4 AUGUST 1857

The yacht *Red Rover* has been on two or three voyages this summer and is now on a cruise in Scotland.

4 APRIL 1859

Shipwreck, the *William* of Newcastle, Captain Turner of this port, which sailed from hence last week, struck a rock last Friday during a gale of wind and was lost. The crew was saved by their own boat.

TO 7 NOVEMBER 1859

Arrived *Laurel* Green & *Violet* Green from Goole with coals.

Sailed *M. & S. Marsden* Knott, *Breeze* Vine, *Auroa* Crooks, *Sarah* Enderby, *Joseph & Ann* Levesley & *Billow* Euder, all to the North & Humber in ballast.

TO 30 JANUARY 1860

Arrived *Breeze* Vine from Newcastle.

TO 20 FEBRUARY 1860

Sailed *Breeze* Vine to Newcastle with mangolds and carrots.

TO 20 FEBRUARY 1860

Windbound. *Neptune, Laurel, Eagle, Victoria, Joseph and Elizabeth, Providence, Sarah, Hopewell* & *Wellington* to the North in ballast.

TO 13 AUGUST 1860

Sailed *Auroa* Vine for London with wheat.

MAY 1861

The new yacht belonging to Henry Bugg Esq., *Sylph,* has arrived off Fosdyke and is much admired, Capt. G. Levesley from Southampton in ballast.

Shipwreck Society

To Capt. Richardson and one crew £4-5s for clothes after the ship *Ebrun* was wrecked off Dunkirk.

£5-7s to the widow of Edward Turner, seaman, who died suddenly on board the schooner *Billow.*

TO 24 AUGUST 1861

Arrived *Perlaw* Pick from Soderham with Deals. *Droning Maria* Nielson from Riga with oil cakes. *Ann* Watson & *John & Ann* Woodward from Goole with coals. *Friends* Greenhall with beach shingle.

Sailed *Providence* Goodeir to South Shields in ballast. *Providence* Ellis to Lynn light. *Providence* Dishman to Grimsby with Wheat. *Elizabeth* Atkin to Seaham in ballast. *Violet* Dunn to Goole light. *Hope* Culpin & *John & Jane* Woodward to beach light. *Herald* Chester to Dunkirk with wheat.

TO 6 DECEMBER 1861

Arrived *Samuel Barnard* Vine (Joseph) from Middlesborough with coals.[1]

TO 14 DECEMBER 1861

Sailed *Samuel Barnard* Vine to Middlesborough in ballast.

TO 4 JANUARY 1862

Arrived *Breeze* Vine (Matthew) and *Samuel Barnard* Vine (Joseph) from Middlesbrough with coals.[2]

---

1 The first report of this vessel in Ships News.
2 The first time Matthew and Joseph Vine arrived together.

12 APRIL 1862
Sailed *London Packet* Vine.

TO 13 DECEMBER 1862
Sailed *Breeze* Vine light for Boston.

TO 10 JANUARY 1863[1]
Sailed *Sarah* Turner to Leith with carrots. *Charles & William* Beleham to Lynn light.

TO 17 JANUARY 1863
Arrived *Samuel* Atkin, *Elizabeth* Atkin, *Violet* Dunn and *Laurel* Green, all from Goole with coals.

TO 7 FEBRUARY 1863
Arrived *Rebecca* Wilson, *Joseph & Ann* Levesley & *M. & S. Marsden* Payne with coals from Middlesborough. *Mark & Elizabeth* Aaron with manure from London. *Neptune* Wilkinson, *Laurel* Green, *Margaret* Watson, *Violet* Dunn all from Goole with coals.

TO 7 FEBRUARY 1863
Sailed *W.R.S.* Culpin & *Hope* Royce to Boston light.

3 OCTOBER 1863
Arrived *Sylph* (yacht) Levesley from Scarborough.

TO 14 NOVEMBER 1863
Arrived *M. & S. Marsden* Payne, *Laurel* Green from Goole with coals. *Breeze* Vine from Boston light. *Violet* Dunn from Grimsby with wood. *Mary Ann* Royce, *Friends* Greenhall & *Samuel* Atkin from the beach with shingle.

TO 11 JUNE 1864
Arrived *Joseph & Ann* Levesley from Goole with coals; *Hope* Royce from Sunderland with coals; *Melita* Hays & *Elizabeth* Atkin both from Middlesborough with coals. *Sarah* Turner from beach with shingle.

---

1 For most of 1863 the majority of the arrivals came from the northern ports of Newcastle and Middlesborough with coals or from Goole with coals from the midland coalfields, for the Spalding gasworks that was built in 1832.

TO 9 FEBRUARY 1867[1]

Arrived *Freedom* Dunn from Hull with oil cakes. *Mary* Purvis from Hartlepool with coals. *Hope* Royce, *Melita* Hayes, *Mary Catherine* Hayes, *Joseph & Ann* Culpin & *Mary & Ann* Royce, all from Goole with coals.
Sailed *Friends* Greenhall to Newcastle with carrots. *Elizabeth* Atkin, *Sarah* Turner, *Betsy* Gleadhill, *Samuel* Atkin all to Lynn light. *W.R.S.* Culpin to Boston light. *Freedom* Dunn to Hull in ballast. *Mary* Purvis to Middlesborough in ballast.

TO 23 FEBRUARY 1867

Sailed *Breeze* Vine to Middlesbrough in ballast. *Mary Ann* Royce to beach light.
Arrived *Laurel* Green, *Freedom* Dunn & *Joseph & Ann* Culpin all from Goole with coals.

TO 8 MAY 1867

Arrived *Breeze* Vine from Hartlepool with coals.

TO 1 FEBRUARY 1868

Sailed *Breeze* Vine to Middlesborough in ballast.

The following vessels sailed in and out of port in 1868: *Freedom* Dunn, *Mary Ann* Dunn, *Friends* Greenhall, *Hope* Royce, *Sarah* Turner, *Elizabeth* Atkin, *Joseph & Ann* Culpin, *Breeze* Vine, *Edward* Payne & *Neptune* Wilkinson.

TO 6 FEBRUARY 1869

Arrived *Neptune* Wilkinson, *Edward* Payne from Goole with coals. *Hope* Royce from Newcastle with coals.
Sailed *Samuel* Atkin, *Mary Ann* Vine, *Agenoria* Smalley, *Joseph & Ann* Culpin, *Neptune* Wilkinson, all to the North in ballast.

TO 17 APRIL 1869

Arrived *Breeze* Vine from Newcastle with coals.

TO 1 MAY 1869

Sailed *Breeze* Vine to the North light.

---

1   Microfilm copies of the *Spalding Free Press* for 1865 and 1866 are not available.

After 1869 there were no more entries of Spalding Ship News found in the *Spalding Free Press*. It is obvious that if the Spalding gasworks (built in 1832) had not needed a supply of coal from the northern and midland coalfields, there would have been little need for any vessels to come up the Welland to Spalding after 1869. Looking through the entries in Spalding Ship News during the previous decade, there were many vessels sailing out in ballast or light to the north and returning with coals.

Spalding gasworks quay under construction. There is a sloop in the foreground, two smaller vessels without masts being used as working platforms, and a ketch behind.

The gasworks quay, February 2013.

10

SPALDING SHIPWRECK SOCIETY

The Spalding Shipwreck Society was formed in 1844 and at one time was one of thirty-three organisations of this type throughout the country. Its purpose was to provide compensation to seagoing members who had suffered shipwreck or other disasters at sea and thereby lost their clothes and other effects. Should loss of life occur, the widow was granted a lifetime's pension or a lump sum in settlement of the same. In the beginning the pension was 1s a week or £10 in settlement. The Ship Albion public house on Albion Street was the society's headquarters for many years, and the club room had pictures of old members decorating the walls into the 1970s. The landlord in 1850, Mr Thomas Draper, was president of the society. (He was father-in-law to my great-grandfather John Henry Vine, who married Rebecca Ann Draper.)

Both Matthew Southwell Vine and Joseph Vine are known to have been early members, and the accounts of the society show that their wives were receiving widows' pensions after their deaths: Hannah Vine from 1878 until 1903, when she died on 7 November, and Mary Vine from 1895 to 1903. From 1879 Hannah Susan Pratt *née* Vine, a sister of Matthew and Joseph, was also receiving a widow's pension. She married her husband John William Pratt, a customs and excise man, in Spalding in 1869. They moved to Hedon, near Hull, where he died in 1874. She returned to Spalding with her two young sons, aged 3 and 1, to live with her mother and became a schoolmistress. Her husband was buried in Spalding cemetery. I am sure John Henry was also a member, having married the daughter of a president of the society. Robert Hutchinson, a ships' engineer and a benefit member, married another of Mr Draper's daughters, Ellen, and at the time of the

1901 census my grandmother Edith Ada Vine (niece) was living with them in Bournemouth and described as a 'mother's help, domestic'.

In 1994, to commemorate its 150th anniversary, M.J. Elsden wrote *A Short History of Spalding Shipwreck Society*, at the end of which was the following paragraph:

> As we approach the 21st Century it is pleasing to see the Shipwreck Society thriving. The Welfare State is such that there is not so much need for a society of this type. Never-the-less so many old traditions and organisations have disappeared, and it would be a pity to see this fine old organisation go the same way as others. With a membership of over 200 the future looks good for the Spalding Society. Although Spalding is no longer a port, many people in the area still earn their livelihood on the High Seas. Life on the sea is a lot safer than it was in years gone by, but accidents do still happen. When a Benefit Member dies either by accident or natural causes their widow still qualifies for the annual Christmas Bonus. Although this is not a large amount it is sufficient for a lady to get herself a little treat, and a reminder that the members of the Society do not forget her.
>
> The Society has survived the last 150 years and we hope and pray that in 150 years' time the membership will still be as active.

Spalding Shipwreck Society Payments Made

From the accounts of the Spalding Shipwreck Society 1867–1903, held at the Spalding Gentlemen's Society:

Payments made to Master Mariners and sailors for loss of possessions:

1867   Robert Atkin, for Clothes lost by the sinking of vessel at Sea, £8-00.
            John Knott, vessel much damaged, partial loss of Clothes, £4-00.

1868   Edward Law, stranded in Brig *John*, partial loss, £4-00.
            William Green & John Collins, *Breeze*, run down at Sea, total loss, £16-00.
            Thomas Royce & Thomas Royce jnr, *Billow*, destroyed by fire, total loss, £16-00.

1870   George Claydon, wrecked in the *Bee*, in 1868, total loss of Clothes, £8-00.

1871   Richard Wright & William Horton, wrecked in the *Urania*, total loss, £16-00.

The boxed compass, dated 1840, that belonged to Captain John Hayes. (Spalding Gentlemen's Society collection)

1872	John Hayes jnr & Richard Wright, for partial loss of Clothes by the sinking of the *Mary Catherine*, £8-00.
1872	George Draper, loss of Clothes by the foundering of the *Craig Ellachie*.
1873	Robinson Duckering, for total loss of Clothes by the foundering of the schooner *Ransom*, £8-00.
	George Claydon, for total loss of Clothes by the part burning & afterwards sinking of the *Happy Return*, £8-00.
1875	W. W. Turner, for partial loss of Clothes by the wreck of the *Western Star*, £6-00.
	William Gosterlow, Joseph Kitchen & Joseph Gosterlow for total loss of Clothes by the wreck of the *Harriet & Eliza*, each £8-00.
1876	G Hill, for total loss of Clothes by the wreck of the *New Unity*, £8-00.
	J. Wilkinson, for total loss of Clothes by the wreck of the *Germ*, £8-00.
1878	Joseph Binks, for total loss of Clothes by the wreck of the *William & Susannah*, £8-00.
1888/89	John Thacker, for total loss of Clothes from barge *Three Sisters*.

11

BOATBUILDERS AND ASSOCIATED INDUSTRIES

Boatbuilders

Many of the larger vessels sailing from Spalding were registered at the Port of Boston. It is likely that most of them would have been built either at Boston or at the larger yards situated around the Humber, and some at Walsoken on the River Nene.

The Protestation Returns for Spalding of 1642 record that Matthew, Robert and William Hakeman had a boatyard (Rose Clark, *Lincolnshire Past and Present* No. 22, winter 1995).

At Boston, Richardson's, Banks', Keightley's, and Goodwin's were boatbuilders. Thomas Goodwin had a boatyard at Spalding on Cowbit Road, across the river from the Welland Inn, where he carried on an extensive trade in small craft, and one at Deeping St James. The boatwright's shop on Cowbit Road was later taken over by his son Richard. In *Pigot's Directory* of 1828 it was in Double Street and later still it was in Marsh Road. This yard was occupied by Mr Richardson in 1848, one of the Richardsons from Boston.

In the 1800s there were two slipways and boatyards by the River Welland on Marsh Road. One of these was owned by Samuel Dring and later by his son Edward Smith Dring; this was the boatyard previously owned by the Goodwins and the Richardsons. The other was owned by John Pannell and was used for hauling up for repairs. Later it was run by his son Ellis Pannell, who in turn was followed by his son John Ellis Pannell. John Ellis died in 1888 and his brother Joseph Ellis returned from Boston to take over the yard.

At a meeting on Monday 17 April 1837, the River Welland Trustees received a memorial from the owners and captains of vessels trading up the River Welland, 'praying the trustees [would] grant to John Panel permission to lay down a slip in the River Welland bank for hauling up vessels for the purposes of repair'. The trustees resolved that 'the desired permission be granted upon such terms as the Clerk shall think advisable and that the slip be laid down under the supervision of the Harbour Master'.

The slip was duly constructed John Pannell. It remained until the time when a new bridge was required over the river because of the volume of road traffic that had increased due to the opening of the sugar beet factory and a site near to the slip was considered to be the best place for it. Mr Pannell did not wish to stand in the way of progress and gave his consent.

1841 Census

Name	Occupation	Address
Henry Morgan	Boat Builder's Apprentice	Albert Street
Richard Wade	Boat Builder's Apprentice	Marsh Gate
John Wade	Boat Builder's Apprentice	Marsh Gate

1851 Census

Name	Occupation	Address
Samuel Dring	Ship Carpenter	Albion Street
John Brown	Ship Carpenter	Marsh Rails Road

1861 Census

Name	Occupation	Address
Samuel Dring	Boatwright	Albion Street
Joseph Ellis Pannell	Boat builder	Marsh Rails Road

1871 Census

Name	Occupation	Address
Samuel J. Dring	Boatwright	Albion Street
John Ellis Pannell	Boat Builder	Marsh Rails Road

1881 Census

Name	Occupation	Address
Samuel Dring	Shipwright	Commercial Road
Henry Morgan	Ship Carpenter	Double Street

Rope Works

There were several rope works at Spalding close to the river. Hemp that was grown in the area between Spalding and Crowland was used for the weaving of rope. Sailing vessels used a large quantity of rope for rigging and hauling up spars and sails. The wear on rope being pulled through pulley blocks meant that it had to be renewed frequently.

In the Protestation Returns for Spalding of 1641, Francis Skellington had a rope works (Rose Clark, *Lincolnshire Past and Present* No. 22, winter 1995).

In Thomas Hawkes' names of the inhabitants of Spalding and their professions in 1792, William Cockett and Ann Hames are listed as rope makers and William Hames as a twine spinner (Spalding Gentlemen's Society).

In *Pigot's Directory* of 1822 the following are listed: Joseph Hames, Holbeach Road; William Hames, Pinchbeck Lane; Robert Winfield, Chain Bridge.

In *White's Directory* of 1826 the following are listed: Hy. and W. Bruff, Cowbit Road; John Fern, Double Street; Joseph Hames, High Street; William Hames, Pinchbeck Street; Benjamin Little, Double Street; Rt Winfield, Chain Bridge.

In *Pigot's Directory* of 1828 the following are listed: John Fern, Double Street; Joseph Hames, Holbeach Road; William Hames, Pinchbeck Street.

In *White's Directory* of 1842 the following are listed: Benjamin Little, James Rogers and William Hames.

In *Slater's Directory* of 1849 the following are listed: Benjamin Little, Marsh Road; William Hames, New Road; Isaac Elsom, Pinchbeck Street.

In the *Post Office Directory* of 1868 the following are listed: Isaac Elsom, New Road; Charles Hames and William Hames, Westlode Street.

In *White's Directory* of 1872 the following are listed: Isaac Elsom, No. 31 New Road; Charles and William Hames, No. 12 Marsh Road.

In *Kelly's Directory* of 1889, the following are listed: Elsom & Son, Pinchbeck Road; William Hames, Marsh Road.

By 1892 George Elsom had taken over from Isaac, and William Hames was still in Marsh Road.

These others listed in the censuses as rope makers were possibly employed at the rope works listed above.

1841 Census

Name	Occupation	Address
James Rogers	Rope Maker	Commercial Road
James Lane	Rope Maker	Marsh Gate

1851 Census

Name	Occupation	Address
Edward Thompson	Rope Maker	Marsh Rails

1881 Census

Name	Occupation	Address
Richard Day	Rope Spinner	Commercial Road

1891 Census

Name	Occupation	Address
George Lill	Rope Maker	Albert Street

Sailmakers

A sailmaking manufactory was started in Spalding as early as 1742, but the location of this early works is not known.

There was a sailmaker listed in the 1826 directory: 'John Best, sail maker private residence, High Bridge.'

In *Pigot's Directory* of 1828, John Best, High Street, was listed.

In *White's Directory* of 1842, Henry Gustard, Holbeach Road, was listed.

In *Slater's Directory* of 1849, Benjamin Lever, sailmaker and ship's chandler, High Street, was listed.

In the 1851 census, William Jackson, sailmaker, 'behind Holbeach Road', was listed.

In *White's Directory* of 1856, Benjamin Lever, waterproof cover and sailmaker and ship's chandler, High Street, was listed.

The blacksmith's shop in the High Street is preserved as a living museum.

Blacksmiths

The account books of Edward Fisher, blacksmith, were found by Mr Geoff Dodd, whose grandfather succeeded Edward Fisher at his premises close to the old Chain Bridge. It is obvious from looking at these accounts that many of the captains and owners of vessels needed the blacksmith for repairs. Works listed in the accounts include 'hoop to water cask', 'new shackle to anchor bowsprit gammon' (the bow fitting that clamps the bowsprit to the stem), 'part new winch repairing', 'chain mended', 'shaft making and alteration to gudgeons' (metal fittings attached to the transom that the pintle rudder fittings fit into), 'boom crutch straightened', 'hoop to mast', 'new shoe to gib stay', 'put on new end to winch handle', 'new boat hook' and many more.

In the years 1826 and 1828–29, the blacksmith in High Street was Francis South. Previous to him was Joseph Rose, who possibly established the premises around 1800. The above-mentioned account books were from 1850, and Edward Fisher continues to be listed in directories in 1868, 1872, 1885 and 1889. In the next directory, *Kelly's Directory* of 1905, William Dodd is listed as blacksmith, High Street.

Other blacksmiths with shops close to the river who may have done work for shipowners were as follows.

Pigot's Directory 1828

Name	Occupation	Address
Thomas Nowell	Blacksmith	Double Street
John Tye	Blacksmith	Near High Bridge

1841 Census

Name	Occupation	Address
Thomas Nowell	Blacksmith	Willow Row
William Rose	Blacksmith	Commercial Road
William Nowell	Blacksmith	Commercial Road
Henry Hutchinson	Blacksmith Apprentice	Commercial Road
Laban Leader	Blacksmith Apprentice	Commercial Road
William Seaton	Blacksmith Apprentice	Commercial Road
Samuel Gilbert	Blacksmith	Albion Street
Robert Cotton	Blacksmith	Albion Street

1851 Census

Name	Occupation	Address
Edward Keightley	Blacksmith	Holbeach Road
Adam Franklin	Blacksmith	Holbeach Road
Henry Cope	Blacksmith	Holbeach Road
William Turner	Blacksmith	Holbeach Road
Robert Wiffen	Journeyman Blacksmith	Holbeach Road

1861 Census

Name	Occupation	Address
Edward Fisher	Blacksmith	High Street
William Fisher	Blacksmith	High Street
Adam Franklin	Blacksmith	Holbeach Road
James Herring	Blacksmith	Holbeach Road
William Turner	Blacksmith	Holbeach Road
William Christian	Blacksmith	Willow Row

Post Office Directory 1868

Name	Occupation	Address
William Turner	Blacksmith	Commercial Road

1871 Census

Name	Occupation	Address
Edward Fisher	Master Blacksmith	High Street
Charles Fisher	Assistant Blacksmith	High Street
Enos Lill	Blacksmith Apprentice	Holbeach Road
George Gardner	Master Blacksmith	Holbeach Road
Henry Sandall	Assistant Blacksmith	Holbeaczh Road
John T. Fox	Master Blacksmith	Holbeach Road
Robert S Marsh	Blacksmith	Holbeach Road
Joseph Harrison	Blacksmith Apprentice	Back Lane

White's Directory 1872

Name	Occupation	Address
John Thorpe Fox	Blacksmith	Holbeach Road
John Senior	Blacksmith	Herring Lane
Edward Fisher	Blacksmith	High Street

1881 Census

Name	Occupation	Address
William Watford	Blacksmith	Double Street (Nag's Head)
Edward Fisher	Blacksmith	High Street
William Fisher	Blacksmith	High Street
William Turner	Blacksmith	Commercial Road

Kelly's Directory 1885

Name	Occupation	Address
William Maxwell	Blacksmith	Commercial Road
William Henry Turner	Blacksmith	Commercial Road

1891 Census

Name	Occupation	Address
Edward Fisher	Blacksmith	High Street
Alfred Watkins	Retired Blacksmith	Albert Street
George Brummitt	Blacksmith	Willow Row Walk

Harbour Masters

The Harbour Master was responsible for keeping the vessels in order and for enforcing the regulations of the river in order to ensure the safety of navigation and the security and correct operation of the port facilities. (See Chapter 2 on the Welland Navigation Laws.)

Year	Name	Address
1834	Samuel Capps	
1839	John Johnson	
1841 (census)	Joseph Dunn	Commercial Road
1848	William Gosterlow	
1851	William White	Holbeach Road
1861	William White	Holbeach Road
1871	Thomas Steadman	Albert Street
1881–1905	Joseph Atkin	Marsh Road
1919–26	John Edward Turner	Double Street
1926–48	George Dodd	High Street

Marine Stores or Chandlers

The mariners would purchase ordinary goods from a variety of shops but the more specialist items needed for use at sea would be purchased from marine stores or chandlers.

In 1642 John Pell and William Wragg are chandlers.

In 1849 Benjamin Lever, sailmaker, is also a ships' chandler.

There were three of these in directories in 1868 and 1872: George Flynn, Mrs Eliza Pannell and Charles Rose.

In the 1871 census, Edmund Carter is listed as a Marine Store Dealer in Holbeach Road.

Wharfingers

A wharfinger is a person who owns or has charge of a wharf.

In 1792 John and William Lamb were wharfingers in Double Street.

Pigot's Directory of 1822 lists Mills, Johnson & Co., Crackpool Lane, as Warfingers.

Pigot's Directory of 1828 lists Jas Back, Double Street, as a Wharfinger.

Slaters's Directory of 1849 lists wharfingers John Moats, Double Street, and Benjamin Addenbrook Mossop, Albion Street.

Wharf or River Porters

These were the persons employed by the merchants or shipowners to unload and load the vessels when they arrived in port.

1851 Census

Name	Occupation	Address
Richard Glenn	Wharf Porter	Holbeach Road
John Cope	Wharf Porter	Holbeach Road
George Sly	Wharf Porter	Holbeach Road
John Forth	Wharf Porter	Holbeach Road

1861 Census

Name	Occupation	Address
James Munton	River Porter	Marsh Road

1871 Census

Name	Occupation	Address
Robert Smith	River Porter	Holbeach Road
Alfred Presgrave	River Porter	Holbeach Road

Customs and Excise

Customs and Excise had the power under the laws of the land at the time to search any vessel arriving in port, to make sure they were not carrying any goods that they had not declared. There were taxes on certain goods entering or leaving the country and as such customs officers could supervise the loading and unloading of goods. There were taxes on wine, brandy, gin, rum, tea, coffee, tobacco and textiles such as silk, lace, muslin and calico, to name a few.

Pigot's Directory 1828

Name	Occupation	Address
William Albin	Coast Waiter of Customs	
? Lansdown	Excise Officer	Double Street

| William Matthews | Excise Officer | New Road |
| Gilbert Young | Principal Coast Waiter of the Customs | Broad Street |

Post Office Directory 1868

Name	Occupation	Address
Andrew Anderson	Principal Coast Officer and Collector of Customs	Commercial Road

Boat Haulers

Many of the vessels had to be hauled up the river when the wind was not favourable.

George Smith of Holbeach Road is listed in 1872 as a higgler and boat hauler.

A 'higgler' in South Lincolnshire dialect meant a person in business in a small way, who perhaps had a horse, a cart and plough to do work for others. Mr Geoff Dodd, in the reminiscences he recorded for 'The Chain Bridge Forge, All Our Stories' collection, told of Jack Cutts, who was a higgler who used to get very drunk on market days. When a pony died it was a tradition to start a little book and solicit the neighbours for a donation to replace it: Jack started up for donations, but never got round to replacing the pony!

12

INTO THE TWENTIETH CENTURY

The end of the nineteenth century had seen a major decline in the number of sailing vessels trading in and out of the River Welland and up and down the east coast. They had for the most part been replaced by steam vessels in the coastal trade, and most of these proved to have been built larger than the river was able to take. There were still some Humber keels and sloops trading in and around the Humber, but these now had steel hulls.

One vessel, the steamship *Mistely*, came up the river with a cargo of 120 tons of manure in January 1908 and went aground just downstream of Pannell's boatyard slipway. Much of the cargo of manure had to be unloaded before it could be refloated and moved up to finish unloading at Chamberlain's Mill in the High Street, opposite Herring Lane (later sold to G. W. Plowman & Son). This vessel remained at Spalding for a month before there was sufficient water in the river to float it to the sea again.

The SS *Misterly* aground in the Welland, January 1908. (F. Parkinson, Spalding Gentlemen's Society Collection)

George Francis Birch senior. (Mrs Margaret Johnson collection)

Messrs Farrow & Sons had two sailing vessels after the First World War, bringing cargoes of war machinery from France.

In 1899, George Francis Birch senior stated that there was still a future for shipping up the Welland, pointing out that it was cheaper to transport the commodities needed by his mill by boat – the cost of shipping from Hamburg to Spalding was 7s 6d while the same cargo by railway from Hull to Spalding cost was 10s.

Birch purchased the *Lizzie and Annie* in 1901, a steam- and sail-powered vessel that was first registered at Lloyd's of London in 1877. In 1916, after a collision with a tug, the *Lizzie and Annie* had its machinery removed and was used as a barge, but after another three years it was converted back to a motor ship. In 1935 more new engines where fitted.

George Francis Birch senior died in 1915 and his son George Francis Birch junior took over the business. G. F. Birch & Co. set up the B. W. Steamship Tug & Lighter Co., and over years acquired a number of boats to transport wheat and other goods to the High Street Mill for use in the manufacture of animal feed. The larger vessels unloaded at their warehouse near Fosdyke Bridge and transferred into barges to be brought up to Spalding.

I remember the workers unloading barges in the High Street in the 1940s, when I lived at No. 4 Commercial Road. We once begged some of the locust bean from them to chew, as sweets were still rationed; it was a rare treat at that time.

George Francis Birch junior named most of his boats after family members. The tugs were *Welshman* (built in 1893 and broken up in 1935) and *Violet Birch*. The cargo ships were *Lizzie and Annie, Mary Birch, Gwendolynne Birch, Margaret Birch* (built by Warren's New Holland yard in 1925), *G.F.B., Yewdale, Buoyant, Yarvik* and *Fosdyke Trader*. The motor barge was *Pride of the Welland*, and the barges were *Agriculture* (sloop-rigged) and *Sarah Birch*.

Barges alongside Birch's warehouse on High Street.

The *Gwendolynne Birch* unloading at Fosdyke. She was built by Warren's New Holland yard in 1923. (Mrs Margaret Johnson collection)

The *G.F.B.* and the *Gwendolynne Birch* at Fosdyke Bridge. (Mrs Margaret Johnson collection)

George Francis Birch junior. (Mrs Margaret Johnson collection)

The tug *Violet Birch* towing the *Agriculture* away from the High Street Mill. (Mrs Margaret Johnson collection)

The motor vessel *Mary Birch* of 157 tons burden, built in 1915. (Mrs Margaret Johnson collection)

The *G.F.B.*
at Fosdyke.
(Mrs Margaret
Johnson
collection)

The *Agriculture*
at Fosdyke.
(Mrs Margaret
Johnson
collection)

The *Mary Birch* was sunk in collision with the trawler *Loch Moidart* in the Humber in 1954. She was subsequently raised and passed into the ownership of R. Lapthorn.

The original Birch's granaries were behind the Fosdyke Bridge on the south-east side. After a fire in the 1930s new buildings were erected on the other side of the river. These eventually became the warehouses used by John Parsons Marketing Ltd, importers of fertiliser. They owned the *Jonsue*, a cargo vessel that came up the Welland regularly until Parsons ceased trading.

In 1908, Mr George Caudwell purchased Wragg Marsh Farm alongside the River Welland, around 2 miles from Fosdyke Bridge on the east side of

Jonsue, 1982.
(By permission
of Mr Neil
Pulling)

Jonsue at
Fosdyke. She
was built
in 1950 at
Terneuzen, the
Netherlands.

the river. Barges travelled to his farm both upstream and down, carrying goods in and agricultural produce out. However, the distance to the nearest wharves proved a problem, so he built one of his own on the riverbank near to Wragg Marsh House. He purchased two small, wooden barges and erected a small derrick that was worked by a horse to load and unload them. He was a pioneer in the use of a light railway on his land, laying a line down to his wharf to transport his potatoes and other produce to be loaded onto the barges and sent onward to market.

A new larger wharf was built in 1915, equipped with a steam crane to replace the original derrick, a small steam tug *Leo* and three larger barges to replace the two wooden ones. This enabled him to transport up to 80 tons of produce at a time to as far away as Boston and King's Lynn and bring back seeds, fertiliser, and coal for his steam engines and for domestic use. Larger coasters were able to bring cargo to the new wharf, and in the 1930s the *Castlerock* was a frequent visitor, bringing in fertiliser from London docks and seed potatoes from Scotland. During the 1930s the *Leo* sank in the river and a firm from Hull was called in to raise it. The operation was successful and it went on to give good service for several more years. (Photographs and some information as produced previously in Stewart E. Squires, *The Lincolnshire Potato Railways*, 1987.)

I used to go with my father to deliver bread to Wragg Marsh Farm when I was on holiday from school during the summer time. Towards the end of the war some of the workers may have been POWs from the camp at Chatterton's Park, Low Fulney, but later in the 1940s they were mostly Irish labourers who lived in huts at the farm. I can remember the railway line being there and the large ramp to the loading dock with flat wagons on it and the line beside the road down to the river next to Lords Drain.

George Francis Birch junior had a younger brother Harold who farmed at Weston and he was one of the first farmers in the area to grow sugar beet. Sometime before 1925 he planted a trial field. When it was harvested the beet was put it into sacks and taken it to Cowhirn, next to the river near Whykam, where it was loaded onto one of Birch's barges and taken to Fosdyke to be shipped over to the factories in Germany. It proved successful and soon became a popular crop in land around Spalding. (Extracted from Margaret Johnson, *History and Photographs of a Spalding Family*, 2009.)

The Spalding sugar beet factory opened in Marsh Road in 1925. The increase in road traffic over the town bridge that it created was a problem, so a new bridge was needed for the traffic bringing the sugar beet from the east side of the river. A site near to Pannell's slipway was thought to be the best place for a new bridge. Mr Pannell was approached and not wanting to stand in the way of progress he consented to this, and his slipway was no longer of any use. He was unable to repair any large vessels anymore, but he carried on building small craft such as the Wildfowler's duck punts, which were called 'shouts' locally. These were used from below Fosdyke at the Welland outfall and all around the coastal marshes of the Wash. They were also used inland when the Cowbit Wash was flooded in the winter. Large bore shotguns know as punt guns loaded and mounted in the shouts would bring down large numbers of wildfowl when discharged.

The small derrick
being worked
by a horse on
the bank of the
River Welland.
(By permission of
Stewart E. Squires)

The larger wharf
at low tide with
the tug *Leo*
and two ladies
bathing. (By
permission of
Stewart E. Squires)

The funnel of
the *Leo* is just
showing to the
left of the barge,
while the steam
crane and its boiler
can be seen in the
top-right corner.
(By permission of
Stewart E. Squires)

The *Castlerock* at the wharf. (By permission of Stewart E. Squires)

Duck punts or shouts on Cowbit Wash. (F. Parkinson, Spalding Gentlemen's Society collection)

The new bridge, named West Elloe Bridge, was built as a lifting drawbridge so that the vessels still coming up the river at high tide were able to pass through.

After John Turner (Harbour Master) had retired from this post, George Robert Dodd, the blacksmith at the Chain Bridge workshop, became the Harbour Master, for which he was paid £5 a year. He also was in charge of the Albert (Chain) Bridge for another £5 a year and a fee of 1s a time from the shipowners for swinging open the bridge for them to pass through. As this was next to the workshop it was very convenient as he would only have to walk round with the winding handle to do this task, but I am not sure how he would know when to do this if boats were coming up fast with the tide.

Geoff Dodd, the last blacksmith, has told me that his father Banks George Dodd (known as Jim, whom I can remember winding the bridge open) told him that sometime after the First World War his father George went away on holiday for a week and left him in charge of the bridge, and he was given the money paid for the opening during that period.

A close up of a shout, showing the large punt gun. (F. Parkinson, Spalding Gentlemen's Society collection)

The *Violet Birch* towing the *Agriculture* through the West Elloe Bridge on its way back downstream to Fosdyke. (Mrs Margaret Johnson collection)

George Robert Dodd, blacksmith and Harbour Master. (Chain Bridge Forge collection)

The *Agriculture* with sails set, from a painting. (Mrs Margaret Johnson collection)

Jim 'Banks' Dodd continued to have the job of opening the bridge until the time when the barges no longer came up the river, but the position of Harbour Master no longer existed; his father George Robert was the last one.

Geoff said his father could remember drawing 30s from Birch's for thirty boats that came up during one month. Sometimes two would come up at a time on a fairly good tide, a flat barge being towed by a motorised one such as the *Pride of the Welland* or the tug boat *Violet Birch*, or just with a couple of men with barge poles to keep them in the middle of the stream and perhaps give them a push now and again. Geoff can only remember seeing a horse towing a barge up the river once, although this had been more common in earlier days when the river was busier.

The only vessel with a mast still coming up the river that Geoff could remember was the *Agriculture*, which did have sails rigged to help the small engine when going out to sea, but I don't suppose it ventured very far along the coast under sail alone.

The last of Birch's ships, named *Empire Fatham*, was built by John Scarr of Hessel in 1944 and launched in 1945. It was bought by the B.W. Steamship Company in 1946 and renamed *Fosdyke Trader*. After leaving for Canada in 1961, it finally finished up a wreck on Seal Island in Nova Scotia around 1991.

My grandparents and parents had been acquaintances of the Dodd family since both families had taken over businesses in the area. George Robert Dodd took over the blacksmith's workshop in 1898 and my grandfather Herbert Seaton acquired the bakery just down the road in Willow Walk in 1901. Grandfather supplied bread to them, and the Dodds would shoe grandfather's pony as well as mending the peel – the tool used to put the bread in and out of the oven. There are many entries in the accounts showing this so it must have worn out quickly.

There were no boats brought up to Plowman's Mill in the High Street after the First World War. This was told to Geoff Dodd by Mr George Plowman.

The wreck of the *Fosdyke Trader* in Nova Scotia.

Left to right: Ralph Seaton (my father), Florence (my mother), Les Freeman, Banks Dodd, Thomas Seaton (my uncle), Herbert Seaton (my grandfather). (Seaton family collection)

I can only remember a few occasions after the Second World War when barges came up river and have no memory of the names of any of the ones that were moored up next to the Black Granary on the High Street opposite Birch's Mill.

After the 1947 flooding along the roads each side of the river, the Coronation Channel was cut around the East side of Spalding from Cowbit Road to Roman Bank and Fulney Lock gates built next to Marsh Road around ½ mile below West Elloe Bridge.

These locks are now only used by an occasional small pleasure boat when they are not silted up.

Some canal barges and others have come from Boston and Wisbech to moor up in town at the time of the Spalding Flower Parade during the last few years as well as a few of the ones from the mooring at the end of the Glen Outfall.

A scheme has been proposed to increase the use of the river for pleasure boating by linking it up with the River Witham via the Glen and the South Forty-Foot Drain and then onwards upstream to another link with the Nene eventually, but I am not sure if this will happen for several years.

Seagoing cargo ships were still coming up the Welland to Fosdyke, to unload cargoes of fertiliser and load other cargo to take away, around the late 1990s. They were small coasters that had to reverse back down the river after unloading. One of these was the Danish vessel *Janne Lindinger*. On its maiden voyage to load wheat it became stuck in the frozen river for six weeks, having waited for a little more cargo instead of going when it could; the skipper was fired on its return to Denmark.

The wharf at Fosdyke is now Fosdyke Yacht Haven for pleasure boats and a few small commercial craft that go out into the Wash with parties of fishermen or for birdwatching cruises organised by the RSPB and Lincolnshire Bird Club.

Fosdyke yacht haven.

Fosdyke yacht haven.

1901 Census

In the 1901 census of Spalding there were still a few local people employed or retired recorded in the Maritime Trades.

Name	Occupation	Address
William Royce	Merchant Seaman	18 Commercial Road
John Wilson	River Porter	18 Commercial Road
John R. Panton	Sailor	18 Commercial Road
Thomas Royce	Sailor	Albert Street
George Nichols	Mariner	Albert Street
Edward Royce	Fisherman	Commercial Road
Robert Naylor	Marine Store	Commercial Road
Robert Hayes	Retired Mariner	Commercial Road
Samuel Culpin	Retired Mariner	Willow Row Walk

Kelly's Directory 1905

Name	Occupation	Address
James Charles Atkin	Master Mariner	Fern Cottage, Albert Street
Joseph Atkin	Harbour Master	13 Marsh Road
Joseph Pannell	Boat Builder	25 Marsh Road

1911 Census

Name	Occupation	Address
James Henry Depear	Seaman (Hay and Corn Merchant Worker)	Albion Street
Henry Dexter Anderson	Bargeman (Corn Merchant Worker)	Albion Street
Thomas Royce	Ship Porter (Hay and Corn Merchant Worker)	Albion Street[1]

---

1 The first three entries in this list were possibly employed by G.F. Birch.

Edward Royce	Sailor	Commercial Road
William Royce	Mariner	Commercial Road
John Hawes Wilson	Boatman (Sailor)	Commercial Road
Freddy C. Stephenson	Master Mariner (Coasting)	Albert Street

Kelly's Directory 1922

James Charles Atkin	Master Mariner	Fern Cottage, Albert Street
John Turner	Harbour Master	Angel Inn, Double Street
Joseph Ellis Pannell	Boat Builder	Marsh Road
E. Smith Dring	Boat Builder	Marsh Road

Kelly's Directory 1926

| John Turner | Harbour Master | 6 Commercial Road |
| Joseph Ellis Pannell | Boat Builder | Marsh Road |

Kelly's Directory 1930, 1933 and 1937

| George Dodd | Harbour Master | High Street |
| Joseph Ellis Pannell | Boat Builder | Marsh Road |

BIBLIOGRAPHY

Benham, Hervey, *Once Upon A Tide* (George G. Harrap & Co. Ltd, 1955).

Burton, Anthony and Clive Coote, *The Past Afloat* (British Broadcasting Corporation/ Andre Deutsch, 1982).

Clapson, Rodney, *A Lincolnshire Shipyard – Burton upon Stather* (Rodney Clapson Publications, 2007).

Ellis, Tony, *Sailing Barges of Maritime England: Little Ships of Our Canals, Rivers and Coasts* (Shepperton Swan Ltd, 1982).

Finch, Roger, *Coals from Newcastle: The Story of the North East Coal Trade in the Days of Sail* (Terence Dalton Ltd, 1973).

Finch, Roger and Hervey Benham, *Sailing Craft of East Anglia* (Terence Dalton Ltd, 1987).

Finden, William and Edward Finden, *Ports and Harbours of Great Britain* (E.P. Publishing Ltd, 1974).

Greenhill, Basil and Ann Gifford, *The Merchant Sailing Ship: A Photographic History* (David & Charles, 1970).

Greenhill, Basil and Ann Gifford, *Victorian and Edwardian Sailing Ships From Old Photographs* (B.T. Batsford Ltd, 1976).

Greenhill, Basil and Ann Gifford, *Victorian and Edwardian Ships and Harbours From Old Photographs* (B.T. Batsford Ltd, 1978).

Gooch, E.H., *A History of Spalding* (The Spalding Free Press Co. Ltd, 1940).

Hedges, A.A.C., *East Coast Shipping* (Shire Publications Ltd, 1974).

Parkin, Dean, *A Maritime Miscellany Volume One: Whitby to Great Yarmouth* (Tyndale & Panda Publishing, 1989).

Roulstone, Alan and Michael Roulstone, *Fenland Waterways* (Balfour Publications (Photo Precision) Ltd, 1974).

Schofield, Fred and Edward Paget-Tomlinson, *Humber Keels and Keelmen* (Terence Dalton Ltd, 1988).

Simper, Robert, *North East Sail: Berwick to King's Lynn* (David & Charles Ltd, 1975).

Sizer, S.M., *Louth Navigation. A History 1756–1926* (Louth Navigation Trust, 1999).

Ulyatt, Michael E., *Flying Sail: Humber Keels and Sloops* (Mr Pye Books, 1995).

Wedgwood, Iris, *Fenland Rivers: Impressions of the Fen Counties* (Rich & Cowan Ltd, 1936).

Wren, Wilfrid J., *Ports of the Eastern Counties* (Terence Dalton Ltd, 1976).

INDEX

Albert Bridge 7, 11, 33–4, 40–1, 43, 53, 132–3, 166–7, 182
Angel Inn 69, 127, 189
Anglo-Saxons 23
Atkin 6, 55, 79–82, 92, 96, 99, 107, 109, 110–12, 114, 119–27, 130, 132, 149, 155–8, 162, 171, 188–9

Barrell, George Francis 40
Bartholomew, John 40
billy–boy 49–52, 102, 120, 133, 135
Birch George Francis jnr 175, 177, 180
Birch George Francis Snr 175
blacksmith 7, 53, 56, 81, 108, 167–70, 182–5
boat hauler 121, 173
boatbuilder 39, 79, 105, 125, 149, 164–65, 188–9
Boston 9, 24, 28, 36–7, 39–40, 43, 45, 54, 56, 64, 70–1, 74–5, 77, 82–3, 85, 88–9, 92, 96, 99, 101, 114–16, 119–21, 123, 139–40, 149, 157–8, 164, 180, 186
Boston Ships Register 54, 75, 78–9, 85–101
Bourne 17, 38–9, 43, 45,
boy (occupation) 54, 72, 75, 77, 116–17
Bugg, Joseph Henry 53, 63–5, 98–9, 110, 131, 136, 154–6
B.W. Steamship Tug & Lighter Co. 175, 185

cabin boy, see boy
Caudwell George 178–80
census 1841 72, 75–6, 103–5, 113, 165–6, 169, 171
census 1851 70, 75, 77, 79, 111–13, 165, 167, 169, 172
census 1861 54, 56, 58, 70, 72, 75, 77, 79–80, 113–18, 165, 169, 172,
census 1862 119
census 1871 69, 71, 74, 77, 79, 81, 113, 119–22, 165, 169–72
census 1872 122,
census 1881 56, 71–4, 76, 79, 81, 113, 123–5, 165, 167, 170
census 1891 56, 65, 71, 74, 76, 81, 100, 113–14, 123–4, 126–7, 167, 170
Chain Bridge, see Albert Bridge
Chain Bridge Forge 53, 108, 167–8, 173, 182–3
chandler (also marine store) 130, 167, 171, 188
Chester 55, 74, 81, 94, 98, 101, 107, 118–19, 123, 130, 147–8, 152, 156
Cook, Captain James 66
Coronation Channel 17, 20–1, 186
Cowbit Wash 14–16, 22, 26, 30, 180, 182
Cox, Thomas 36
Culpin family 55, 72–73, 81, 87, 90, 95, 100, 105, 107,

109–11, 115–18, 121, 130, 132, 139–42, 144–7, 150, 152, 155–8, 188
customs 28, 40, 42, 64, 113–14, 130, 132, 161, 172–73
Cutts, Jack 173

Danes 24–5, 46
Defoe, Daniel 36–37
Dictionary of the World 1772 36
Discovery, HMS 66–8
Dodd 7, 53, 108, 167–8, 171, 173, 182–6, 189
Drakard's *Stamford News* 137–8
Draper family 57, 59, 78–79, 86–7, 92, 95–6, 105, 107–8, 110–11, 119, 139–48, 161, 163

Elsden, M.J. 162

fen lighters 30, 34–5, 37, 43–6, 82, 116, 133–4
Fisher, Edward, ledger of 53, 56, 63, 80–1, 108–11, 167–8
flooding 8, 12, 14–17, 22, 24, 26, 31, 37, 42, 180, 186
Fosdyke Bridge 21, 38–9, 70, 114–15, 129, 149, 151, 175–6, 178

gasworks 40, 73, 133, 157, 159–60
Gazetteer of the British Isles 40

G.F. Birch & Co. 7, 175, 188
Glen, River 9, 12, 17, 21, 27, 38, 43–5, 82, 186
Gooch, E.H. 27, 32, 36, 64, 67, 126, 133, 136
Gosterlow 55, 71–3, 76, 87–8, 90, 93, 97–8, 108–10, 112, 122–4, 127, 130, 133, 138–46, 150, 152–3, 155, 163, 171
Grassam 58–62, 79, 125–7
Grundy, John jnr 43, 82–4

harbour masters 40–2, 68–9, 72, 80, 111, 118, 122, 124, 165, 170–1, 182–4, 188–9
Harmstone, Robin 38–9
Hawkes, Thomas 37–8, 166
Hayes 6, 55, 75–6, 81, 89, 91, 99–100, 105, 108, 110, 114–16, 118, 122–3, 127, 147, 158, 163, 188
higgler 79, 173
High Bridge 21, 23, 27, 32, 38, 40–2, 134–5, 167–8
History and Photographs of a Spalding Family 180

keel 46–7, 50, 83, 96, 114, 123, 174,
Kelly's Directory 1885 57, 81, 125, 170
Kelly's Directory 1889 125, 166,
Kelly's Directory 1905 168, 188
Kelly's Directory 1922–37 189
Knott 76–78, 87, 95, 108, 115, 117–18, 120, 130, 137, 150, 152, 155, 162

Levesley 6, 53, 63–6, 81, 93, 98, 100, 103, 108, 111, 115, 118–19, 122–5, 131, 136, 147–8, 153–8
lighter, see fen lighter
Lincoln, Rutland & Stamford Mercury 41, 53, 137, 146–9
Lincolnshire in 1836 146
Lincolnshire Past and Present 164, 166

Lincolnshire Potato Railways, The 180
Lords Drain 31, 43, 180

malt trade 29–30, 37,
marine store, see chandler
Moorsom rule 85

Navy 61, 66–8
Nene, River 14, 22, 26, 30, 37, 164, 186

Pannell, J.E. 135–6
Pannell's boatyard 107, 133, 135–6, 164–5, 174, 180
Perry, Captain John 30, 38–9
Pigot's Directory 1822 166, 171
Pigot's Directory 1828 164, 166–9, 171–2
Post Office Directory 1868 55, 119, 166, 169, 173
Protestation Returns 164, 166

railway 13, 17, 39, 45, 126, 148–50, 175, 179–80
river porters 135, 172, 188
regatta 64–5, 154
Roman Bank 21–3, 186
Romans 10–11, 22–3, 27, 43, 46
rope makers (also rope works) 39, 166–67
Royal Navy, see Navy
Royce 55, 68–71, 81, 86, 89–91, 94–6, 98–101, 104, 108–11, 115, 117–22, 124–5, 127, 130–1, 138–45, 147–8, 150–1, 157–8, 162, 188

sailmakers 167, 171
Ship Albion 57, 78–9, 161
shipbuilder, see boatbuilder
Short History of Spalding Shipwreck Society, A 162
Slater's Directory 1849 107, 166–7, 171
sloop 46–51, 54, 64, 66, 70–2, 74–5, 77–83, 85–102, 108–11, 114–15, 119–124, 126, 151, 159, 174–5

Smalley, Mrs 133–5
smuggling 64, 130
Spalding Free Press 40, 53, 55, 66, 77, 130, 149–60
Spalding Gentlemen's Society 82, 162
Spalding Shipwreck Society 57, 66, 68, 71, 75, 78, 81, 156, 161–63
Stamford 7, 9–12, 24, 28–9, 34, 37, 40, 91
Stamford Canal 7, 11–12, 82
Stamford Herald & County Chronicle 138–46
sugar beet factory 165, 180

Turner 55, 66–70, 81, 92–5, 98, 101, 110, 112, 119, 121, 123–5, 127, 129–32, 138–143, 145–6, 151, 153, 155–8, 163, 169–71, 182, 189
Turner, Mrs 64, 67–8, 72–3, 79, 130–33

Vermuyden, Sir Cornelius 30
Victoria Bridge 32–3, 35, 40
Vikings, see Danes
Vine 6, 8, 53–7, 59, 63, 76, 79, 89, 92–4, 97, 99, 101, 104, 108–10, 112, 114–15, 117–19, 121–5, 130, 133, 147–8, 150, 152–9, 161–2

Welland Navigation Bylaws 41–2, 170
West Elloe Bridge 182–3, 186
Westlode, the 22, 26, 31, 39, 43
wharf porters, see river porters
wharfingers 40, 171
White's Directory 1826 166
White's Directory 1842 75, 105, 166, 167
White's Directory 1856 54, 107–8, 167
White's Directory 1872 55, 74, 122–3, 166, 170
White's Directory 1892 81, 127